W9-DCN-856

The Librarian's Guide to WordPerfect 5.0

Supplements to
COMPUTERS IN LIBRARIES

1. Essential Guide to dBase III+ in Libraries
   Karl Beiser
   ISBN 0-88736-064-5   1987   CIP

2. Essential Guide to Bulletin Board Systems
   Patrick R. Dewey
   ISBN 0-88736-066-1   1987   CIP

3. Microcomputers for the Online Searcher
   Ralph Alberico
   ISBN 0-88736-093-9   1987   CIP

4. Printers for Use with OCLC Workstations
   James Speed Hensinger
   ISBN 0-88736-180-3   1987   CIP

5. Developing Microcomputer Work Areas
   in Academic Libraries
   Jeannine Uppgard
   ISBN 0-88736-233-8   1988   CIP
   ISBN 0-88736-354-7 (softcover)

6. Microcomputers and the Reference
   Librarian
   Patrick R. Dewey
   ISBN 0-88736-234-6   1988   CIP
   ISBN 0-88736-353-9 (softcover)

7. Retrospective Conversion:
   A Practical Guide for Libraries
   Jane Beaumont and Joseph P. Cox
   ISBN 0-88736-352-0   1988   CIP

8. Connecting with Technology 1988:
   Microcomputers in Libraries
   Nancy Melin Nelson, ed.
   ISBN 0-88736-330-X   1989   CIP

9. The Macintosh ® Press: Desktop
   Publishing for Libraries
   *Richard D. Johnson and
   Harriett H. Johnson*
   ISBN 0-88736-287-7   1989   CIP

10. Expert Systems for Reference and
    Information Retrieval
    Ralph Alberico and Mary Micco
    ISBN 0-88736-232-X   1990   CIP

11. EMail for Libraries
    Patrick R. Dewey
    ISBN 0-88736-327-X   1989   CIP

12. 101 Uses of dBase in Libraries
    Lynne Hayman, ed.
    ISBN 0-88736-427-6   1990   CIP

13. FAX for Libraries
    Patrick R. Dewey
    ISBN 0-88736-480-2   1990   CIP

14. The Librarian's Guide to WordPerfect 5.0
    Cynthia LaPier
    ISBN 0-88736-493-4   1990   CIP

15. Technology for the 90's
    Nancy Melin Nelson, ed.
    ISBN 0-88736-487-X   1990   CIP

16. Microcomputer Management and
    Maintenance for Libraries
    Elizabeth S. Lane
    ISBN 0-88736-522-1   1990   CIP

17. Public Access CD-ROMS
    in Libraries:
    Case Studies
    *Linda Stewart, Kathy Chiang,
    Bill Coons, eds.*
    ISBN 0-88736-516-7   1990   CIP

18. The Systems Librarian's Guide to
    Computers
    Michael Schuyler, ed.
    ISBN 0-88736-580-9   1990   CIP

19. Essential Guide to dBase IV in Libraries
    Karl Beiser
    ISBN 0-88736-530-2   1990   CIP

20. Essential Guide to UNIX in Libraries
    D. Scott Brandt
    ISBN 0-88736-541-8   1990   CIP

21. Integrated Online Library Catalogs
    Jennifer Cargill, ed.
    ISBN 0-88736-675-9   1990   CIP

22. CD-ROM Retrieval Software:
    An Overview
    Blaine Victor Morrow
    ISBN 0-88736-667-8   1991   CIP

23. CD-ROM Licensing and Copyright Issues
    for Libraries
    *Nancy Melin Nelson and Meta Nissley,
    editors*
    ISBN 0-88736-701-1   1990   CIP

24. CD-ROM Local Area Networks:
    A User's Guide
    Norman Desmarais, ed.
    ISBN 0-88736-700-3   1990   CIP

25. Library Technology 1970-1990:
    Shaping the Library of the Future:
    Contributions from the 1990
    Computers in Libraries Conference
    Nancy Melin Nelson, ed.
    ISBN 0-88736-695-3   1990   CIP

26. Library Technology for Visually and
    Physically Handicapped Patrons
    Barbara T. Mates
    ISBN 0-88736-704-6   1991   CIP

27. Local Area Networks in Libraries
    Kenneth Marks and Steven Nielsen
    ISBN 0-88736-705-4   1991   CIP

The Librarian's Guide to WordPerfect 5.0

Cynthia B. LaPier

Meckler

Westport • London

Library of Congress Cataloging-in-Publication Data

LaPier, Cynthia B.
    The librarian's guide to Wordperfect 5.0 / Cynthia B. LaPier.
      p. cm. -- (Supplements to computers in libraries ; 14)
    Includes bibliographical references.
    ISBN 0-88736-493-4 (alk. paper) : $
    1. Word processing -- Library applications.   2. WordPerfect
(Computer program) 3. Library administration--Data processing.
4. Libraries--Automation.   I. Title. II. Series.
Z678.93.W67L36   1990
652.5 ' 536--dc20   89-49457
                                          CIP

British Library Cataloguing in Publication Data

LaPier, Cynthia B.
    The librarian's guide to wordperfect 5.0.
    1. word processing
    I. Title   II. Series
    652 . 5

    ISBN 0-88736-493-4

Copyright © 1990 Meckler Corporation. All rights reserved.
No part of this publication may be reproduced in any form
by any means without prior written permission from the publisher,
except by a reviewer who may quote brief passages in review.

Meckler Corporation, 11 Ferry Lane West, Westport, CT 06880.
Meckler Ltd., Grosvenor Gardens House, Grosvenor Gardens,
   London SW1W 0BS, U.K.

Printed on acid free paper.
Printed and bound in the United States of America.

This work is for my sons,
Jason, thank you for letting me use the computer,
Benjamin, thank you for learning how to cook.

CONTENTS

Part 1:
The Function Keys

Part 2:
Creating Documents

INTRODUCTION

WordPerfect, a wordprocessing program from WordPerfect Corporation, is one of the top selling software programs in the PC world. The most popular of recent versions, 5.0 offers the user the opportunity to combine graphics with text, as well as all the other standard word processing features. The text format is not limited in sophistication by the program, indeed format is limited only by the user's imagination.

It is true that just as we master one version of a piece of software, a newer, better, faster, revised and updated version arrives on the scene. During the editing of this volume, WordPerfect version 5.1 was released. However, this latest version of WP is not dramatically different from 5.0 and all the functions in the following pages are applicable to this most recent release. As long as new versions remain within the 5._ family, then the changes are not all-encompassing. For example, the change from 4.2 to 5.0 included graphics, fonts, and styles, just to name a few of the affected features. The changes in 5.1 are improvements, but are not major ones. I have noted some of them at the end of this introduction.

Librarians have always had a less than positive image; and it is true that a positive first impression is the most important. With WP 5.0, librarians can create first impressions through documentation that will attract a patron to a bibliography or a pathfinder, that will appeal to a Board member, that will make a legislator or fund-giver at least notice an appeal before it is tossed. WP makes uploading and downloading files from other sources easier. The librarian can consider the possibility of giving a patron a downloaded search on his own disk and re-formatted in WP; and if really creative and ambitious, the librarian can index the file in WP. Finally, the librarian has the opportunity to explain to the patron ways to manipulate the citations to his advantage.

This book offers the librarian user details on getting around in the program; and it offers examples for supervisors who might not use the program yet but who do expect staff members to use it and use it well. The examples will help the supervisor motivate staff to be more creative, they will help the supervisor to see what is possible, to know whether the staff has reached the limits of the program. The examples will also help the user get to the end product quickly and fairly painlessly during the learning process.

Most librarians will admit that drab and unattractive documents have often been usually commonplace. These productions in library-type institutions are the direct result of lack of funds to contract with a graphics artist and/ or a print shop. WP eliminates the need for out-of-house jobs in many cases.

Graphics is used to mean clip art, designs, borders, and any horizontal or vertical lines that are added to a page for effect, emphasize, or to provide further information. WP 5.0 allows the insertion of any of these features directly on a page right from the screen; in other words, without the necessity for glue and scissors. Some of these features may be used infrequently, and none of them should be overused; but they are all effective and are definitely worth considering.

In the old days most of us had access to one typewriter with one type of print. Even with the advent of electronic-memory typewriters, we were still restricted to a very few different types of print styles. Bitstream has provided WP 5.0 owners, at no cost, an installation kit and three typefaces: Dutch, Swiss, and Charter. The user has the option of which typefaces are to be installed on the computer, as well as the point sizes in these typefaces in italics or bold, landscape or portrait. The only limitation is the amount of space available on the fixed disk. When the user inserts a code for a particular font within the text, during the print process, the font is downloaded to the printer memory so that the font of choice is printed. This is considered a soft font as opposed to a cartridge font which is an actual plastic cartridge that fits in the front slot of the printer. Of course, there are many additional fonts available for purchase from other vendors. Because it is assumed that most libraries are on limited budgets, and that the only fonts that will be available will be the free ones, the discussion in this book will be confined to the Bitstream font options.

Two different versions of a document can be compared with each other, one on the screen, the other saved on a disk. This is useful to trail edits and revisions when writing the great American novel.

References to other pages or to figures are much like SEE and SEE ALSO's; they are created automatically, as if by the Library of Congress. They can be placed anywhere on the page, in footnotes, headers or footers, or within graphics. The neatest feature is that they will be updated automatically during the editing process. No matter how much text is inserted or deleted, the reference page numbers can be generated at any time to reflect the current document accurately.

To refer once again to the typewriter era, when we wanted to advance up or down a page, a half space or many spaces, or across the page, we used the roller thing and the space bar. WP 5.0 allows a much more accurate and scientific placement on the page. Instead of inserting hard returns to scroll down a page or the space bar to move text over on a line, an advance position command is used to place text exactly where the creator desires.

The characters visible on the keyboard are not the only ones available to the user. There are other sets limited only by the capabilities of the printer. The sets contain symbols and graphics, fractions, and other weird things to put on a page. Some of the infamous cataloguing eccentricities (^, é, ¶) become readily available through character sets. WP has included a test document (charmap.tst) which, when printed, will display the characters available for the chosen printer, Whatever appears on the printed page will be created using the table location and the compose function.

Although the speller and thesaurus are in one language, American English, WP 5.0 gives an option of the language code in which the document will be written. Libraries that create bilingual documents of any kind will find this to be advantageous. Of course, the languages for which WP 5.0 sells additional dictionaries and thesauruses are the Romance and Scandinavian languages, but with multiple requests from librarians we may be able to prove the viability of dictionaries based on Arabic, African, Indian, and Oriental languages.

A Master Document is created from several subdocuments which, taking a book as an example, might be the table of contents, the chapters, and an index. The advantage of using this feature is that dealing with smaller files throughout the creation process, and combining everything in one step at the end is a much more efficient work process. The various option codes, which are used to set up page formatting features, can be stored in the master document or in each subdocument. For the very long project or the multi-authored project, this is definitely advantageous.

If the computer in use has a graphics card, the user can preview the entire page, graphics and text, before printing. This is most useful for an overall look at layout, but it is not intended to be scanned for textual content. It certainly saves wear and tear on a laser printer. In a machine with turbo speed, preview takes only seconds, definitely faster than printing a page to see what you will get.

WP 5.0 has included a screen capture program that works externally to capture graphics from any compatible graphics program. The program saves the screen image to a file that can then be incorporated into a WP document.

THE WP APPROACH

There are two ways to approach WordPerfect command features; either through a numeric key choice from a menu, or an alpha key (usually mnemonic) from the same menu. The user can intermingle these without conflict, but it is easier to develop a consistent pattern. Both numeric and alpha command keys are discussed throughout this book. In reality, a mixture of both types will probably be the preferred method.

Command codes to change format or text characteristics are imbedded and hidden from the user's sight. The REVEAL CODES, ALT-F3 command shows the codes in their symbolic form. The only way to remove most codes after they have been created is to use REVEAL CODES and remove them from that window. This is the most important feature for successful use of WP. Entering several codes for one feature, for instance margins, confuses not only the user but the program. When users have problems with WP, a look at the codes usually will immediately show the cause, which will be that either too many codes have been used or that the wrong codes altogether have been used. It is a very useful habit to work with codes revealed at all times on the screen. At first this disconcerts many users, but in the long run and over time, users will wonder how they ever survived without looking at the codes all of the time.

WHEN TO USE AND WHEN NOT TO BOTHER

Every time a librarian completes an action that is repeated more than once the use of the computer is appropriate. Form letters, overdue notices, thank you notes, invitations, meeting agendas, annual reports, letters of inquiry, new book notices, and workshop evaluations are all items that change very little from one time to the next. The entire document can be stored on the fixed disk, ready to be retrieved at a moment's notice for an instantaneous need. The date is entered by code so that it always appears as the current date, and the *revised* information can then be entered. For items that are repeated but change in content (annual reports should fall in this category but in reality I am willing to bet that they do not), memos, press releases, newsletters, meeting minutes, registration forms, a format file is set up with the unchanging information located where it will appear in the final document. Both of these types of files can be created as templates, merge files, or macros, depending upon the time, interest and expertise of the librarian. The most important point is that if the librarian spends time doing any action more than once, that librarian should look to a more efficient way to complete the action by repeating as little as possible and by using past actions as a basis for current and future actions. We understand how to automate the card catalog, but we often fail to see that the same automation techniques can be used in office routines and document production.

A good time not to use WP is when filling out forms. It is very possible to set up a file to place the text exactly on the page where the form fill-in is located, but it is, quite frankly, not worth the time and energy to figure out where things go. It is easier to either retype the entire document as a template on which to enter the information, or go back to the good ole' typewriter squirreled away in the cataloguing office. Typing any kind of 3 x 5 or 5 x 8 card, unless the librarian is using form feed cards, will also be easier with a typewriter. Again, it is possible to do this, but especially with a laser printer, it may prove not to be worth the hassle of setting up the file to work correctly.

If printing envelopes infrequently, perhaps the odd letter for which you do not have a set of address labels already printed, it is possible to block the address portion of a letter, and copy to a second document file, and then print on an individual envelope. This is useful for a once in awhile need. If the intention is to print hundreds of envelopes, the computer will not be effective unless there is an envelope feeder bin attached to the printer.

UBIQUITOUS FUNCTIONS

Ubiquitous functions are much like ubiquitous bibliographic records; they can be found everywhere, are not unique to any situation, and have already been done once by someone somewhere.

Some of WP's features are useful for all professions, but little library profession quirks are rewarded by the effectiveness of WP. For instance, many of us tend to use the year/month/day format, yrmoda (890531) which is unknown outside of computer and military circles. With the date format possibilities in WP, it is quite feasible to set up the default date, so that it will always print in that particular format.

The concordance index function is a marvelous tool but especially so for the library world. One concordance index file can be created for all meeting minutes, five year plans, policy and procedure manuals. Then each document will be indexed on the same terms, the same set of keywords resulting in a standardized document format for the institution. Some keywords will not appear in all documents, but there will be a set of words or phrases which will be important in all cases where they exist. It will not be necessary to recreate this subject list for every publication. It is even feasible that the list be selected by a group of professionals to, again, maintain that consistency that librarians do so love. The possibilities are even more extensive when one considers that all documents published during the year can be combined into a master document which will be indexed with the agreed-upon concordance. For instance, if all board agendas and minutes were to be combined into one final year-end publication and then indexed, not only would access be greatly improved, but the professionalism of the organization would be reflected in the final report.

The merge function is typically used to merge form letters with addresses. Although this is a viable need in a library institution, there are many other possibilities for merge. If a base file is created of a bibliographic record, then it can be used later to produce a new book list, an annotated bibliography for a faculty member, catalog cards (if one is still doing cards), a report on coordinated collection development, an annual acquisitions list, subject bibliographies, pathfinders, a column in the campus newspaper, a budget report, a list for a gift giver. Any time the bibliographic record is used, it will not have to be rekeyed; the original entry will serve all needs. All needs can be sorted on chosen fields and alphabetized as desired. Lists could be created according to author, title, or copyright date. Subject headings can be created as a field for subject sorts.

In libraries where the budget is small, less than, say, $100,000, it is possible to maintain simple files with WP. The main ledger may be in a spreadsheet, this is a personal choice; but it is possible to keep budget figures in a merge file format. This file can then be merged into a file with math columns defined, and can be sorted in a variety of ways. For instance, by budget code, by area (supplies or equipment), by vendor, by type of material purchased (books, periodicals, software), by date, by amount. Lists can be alphabetized before totalling.

The outline feature is useful for establishing action plans, job descriptions, personnel responsibilities, bibliographic instruction lesson plans, transparencies for overheads, policy and procedure manuals, guides for presentations. The outliner is so versatile that one of the default formats can be used or the user can establish a completely different style.

The style feature is much like the style sheet of a desktop publishing program. One style sheet might be created for use by all word processors within a library to create standard headings, newsletter article titles, document titles and subtitles. The use of style is fairly easy even though creating the style itself might be complicated. One *expert* on the staff might invest the time to create a set of styles to be used by those who do not necessarily need or desire to devote the time and energy to do the same thing. Again, anytime that redundancy can be reduced is a time when computers should be used to their utmost.

Many of us are faced with increasing interlibrary loan activities, but no efficient way to maintain statistical data. By creating a merge file for ILL, it is then possible to use that file to create monthly reports of borrowers, lenders, type of item, periodical titles, whatever those who control the purse strings need to know to increase funding. Counting transactions is even a snap, if the line numbering feature is used. Once again, this is most effective for a fairly small operation, and only if keying the ILL data into a record file does not constitute more work than previous manual type record keeping. On the newer and faster machines, the size of the file is not limited. A fast machine can easily manipulate a file of many hundreds of records without causing the librarian to take a two hour lunch break waiting for the machine to finish processing. It is also important to compare the time it takes the computer to generate the reports to the time it took a clerk to do it the old way; it may just be that the old way is the most efficient, although that is unlikely once the procedure is perfected.

WP 5.1

As with any software, the first *edition* is a chancy purchase. It is liable to have bugs to be discovered by the user, corrected by the software publisher, and then redistributed to the user. Any releases after that first one will be fairly safe. This latest version, 5.1, released in November of

1989, is different enough to require some extra hours converting files and re-learning the program. An installation process is required for the first time. The reference manual has been expanded, and its format is quite different to accommodate the additional features and the mouse functions. The program has obviously become more sophisticated and versatile, but be prepared to keep WP 5.0 on the hard disk until the new version has been completely mastered.

Some of the major and worthwhile changes are briefly described below.

Tabs - When a tab is changed, for instance, from center to left alignment, all the tabs in the document are reformatted. It is no longer necessary to go through the document, remove tabs, and re-enter tabs.

Menus - The menus are the pull-down sort and can be mouse controlled. The function keys work as they did before, but this new method of control allows an easier transition for Macintosh people, or any users accustomed to everything being offered on the screen, rather than being stored in one's head.

Ownership - The earlier version which is being replaced by 5.1 can be donated to a school with a complete transfer of the registration. This is a new attitude by a software publisher, and one which we should all encourage.

Tables - Previously tables were not really tables at all, they were tabbed columns. The new method deals with tables as tables.

Justification - This alignment feature has been expanded to include a right alignment and a feature to center paragraphs instead of just single lines.

Font sizes - The set-up feature allows the option of setting exactly what size "extra large", "large", and other font options are instead of depending upon the WP default. In 5.0 the user had to use the PTR function to change these font sizes.

Labels - Creating labels for a laser printer is suddenly a breeze, and a pleasure to do.

Spreadsheet link - It has always been possible to bring spreadsheet data into a WordPerfect document; now it is also possible to establish a link between the spreadsheet and WordPerfect so that the imported information will be updated with the spreadsheet.

Graphics - There are thirty new graphics included, some of which are a certificate, a calendar, a personal computer, a banner, and a printer.

Keyboard - The keyboards options have been expanded. Users can now choose among the typical, the expanded with F11 and F12, a shortcut version, and a macro version. They can be changed according to the need at the time of document creation.

A WORD OR TWO TO THE READER

WP works with mnemonic keys or numeric keys. In cases where both choices are possible, both are discussed. All alpha or numeric characters that are **bolded** within the text represent keys that will actually cause a selection of a particular function or menu option. In some cases the initial letter or a letter within a word may be boldfaced. This means that either the alpha character or the numeric character can be used to select the function.

In our discussions, if two keystrokes are shown in upper case type, and next to one another, the keys should be entered or struck simultaneously. For instance, **ALT F7**, means to hold down the **ALT** key while striking the **F7** key.

Because function keys play a crucial role in a user's understanding and utilization of WordPerfect's features, both basic and advanced, in the first part of this book we will consider each function key in its own chapter, discussing all of the commands in which it is used, both alone and in combination with other keys. A thorough grounding in the uses of function keys will allow the reader to enter the second part of this book with confidence.

In the second part, beginning on page 77, we will explore examples of documents created using WP while furthering our understanding of specific word processing techniques and features.

BASICS

If WordPerfect has not been installed on your computer:

Computer Requirements: It is necessary to have a hard drive, also known as a fixed drive, to run WP. Although there are some intrepids who run the program from a floppy, it is not advisable and certainly not practical. The system should have at least 512K RAM, about 5 MB free on the hard drive, and ideally a graphics card.

Installation: The Learning disk has an installation program. Turn the computer on; at the C prompt, type **A:** and press ENTER and Install and press ENTER. From that point follow the instructions as displayed on the screen exactly. If you try to bypass these steps and do a straight copy from all the floppies which come with WP onto your hard drive, you will not only be wasting your time, you will also be copying additional files which you will never use, for other printers, etc. WP will install the program using the directory WP50; do not change this to WP. It may seem like it will be less to type initially, but later on it will haunt you because so many defaults within the program expect WP50 as the name of the WP *root* directory. After installation, every time you turn on the computer you will enter **CD\WP50** and press ENTER, **WP** and press ENTER.

Printer: The next step is to select a printer. With WP up and running, press **SHFT F7, S, 2 [A]** with the disk labelled Printer 1 in the floppy drive. Move the cursor to the printer which you will be using and press ENTER. EXIT the print menu. This process creates a printer file which will be specific to the type of printer that you have just defined. If you are truly intrepid you can review the information in this file by exiting WP, and running the program PTR followed by the printer file name. For example, enter at the C prompt (but within the WP50 directory), PTR HPLASII.PRS and press ENTER.

CONFIG.SYS: The config.sys file should have a FILES=20 command for WP to run efficiently and to avoid memory problems.

BATCH FILE: A batch file is much like a macro, it allows you to execute a program or a computer event with a reduced number of keystrokes. For instance to create a batch file to start up WP, you might, on a blank WP screen, type the following:

```
cd\WP50        ENTER
WP             ENTER
```

Then using **CTRL F5, 1** DOS TEXT, save the file as WP.BAT. The BAT extension is absolutely necessary, as it tells DOS that this file is a batch file. The next time you want to run WP, all you have to do is enter **WP**. This is the most simplistic version of a batch file, the AUTOEXEC.BAT is another example that should be present on every hard drive. It is important not to save a batch file as if it were a regular WP file. This version of WP adds additional information to the file that is hidden to the user, but is visible to DOS and will prevent the batch file from executing properly. If you load a batch file in WP you may notice a ^Z in the last line. That is supposed to be there. It is an end-of-file marker that, again, is a DOS feature.

CURSOR CONTROL

The cursor is the blinking short line that the user can move anywhere within the document. It is the point of input. The cursor will not go beyond where the user has defined the limits. It will not go beyond the end of the document or into the margins without additional commands. When it moves it does not actually move characters or text or graphics; it simply moves the place of being, not the being itself. As with most computer programs the arrows on the keyboard, either as a separate entity or connected to the numeric pad, are the cursor controls--right, left, up, down.

ADDITIONAL CONTROLS

What every typist never learned, additional controls save much time and should be memorized above all else. What follows is a partial listing of the most basic of these controls.

END will get you to the end of a line immediately.

ESCAPE will allow you to define how far you want to go. Simply hit the **ESC** key, then the number of times to be moved, then the key to define how the movement is to be:

Examples
ESC 4 → moves four characters to the right
ESC 10 PAGE DOWN moves down ten pages.

HOME HOME ↑ goes to the beginning of the document.

HOME HOME HOME ↑ or **HOME HOME HOME** ←
goes to the beginning of the document and places the cursor before all of the embedded codes.

HOME HOME and an **ARROW** key

→	goes to the right margin
←	goes to the left margin
↑	goes to the top of the document, but only to the beginning of the visible text
↓	goes to the end of the document

CTRL-HOME (GO TO function) moves the cursor to a specific position:

CTRL-HOME page number goes to the page specified.

CTRL-HOME-CTRL-HOME turn block on then use this to rehighlight the last block (SEE BLOCK, ALT F4, PAGE 22)

CTRL-HOME→ goes to the next column.

PAGE UP/DOWN does the obvious, goes to the first line of the previous page, or to the top of the next page.

SCREEN MOVERS (-) OR (+) move a screen display up or down. They do not move a whole page. Do not use the - or + that are on the top line of the keyboard, but use the - or + on the numeric pad. The top row of the keyboard is used for creating characters, the numeric pad keyboard is used for control functions, and will not create characters. When NumLock is engaged, the

3

numeric pad keyboard will create numbers on the screen, but this is not practical in word processing.

CTRL-ARROW key moves the cursor a word at a time to the right or to the left, moves the cursor to the beginning of the word. Does not work with the up and down arrow keys.

SPEED--how fast the cursor moves is controlled by the setup **SHFT-F1, 2,** or **SHFT F1, C**. This needs to be established only one time. The default is 30 characters per second. You may adjust this to your typing speed or non-speed, as the case may be. If the cursor does not act properly, there may be an incompatibility problem with another program on your computer, in which case you should choose *normal* as the default speed.

RETURN is also the enter key. Striking **RETURN**, the hard return, is like a carriage return on the typewriter; it takes the typist to the next line. Because WP automatically wraps text around from line end to line beginning, it is not necessary to use the Return key at the end of a line. Instead WP inserts a Soft Return, which just marks the end of a line. To create a Soft Return, use **HOME ENTER**.

SPACE BAR does what it does on a typewriter, it enters spaces. If you want a space to appear between two words, but you want the words to appear together on the same line, use **HOME SPACE BAR** to create a hard space. The space bar also provides an exit from the **HELP** screens.

4

PART 1:
THE FUNCTION KEYS

F1

F1   cancels any command, and allows you to exit gracefully without having effected an execution.

            F1 becomes a restorer of the previously deleted text, after text has been typed and erased with either the backspace or delete key.

SHFT F1   establishes the setup of the program. See Fig.1-1, Setup.

1 Backup (type either **1** or **B**, uppercase or lowercase, to perform the function) makes an automatically timed backup of the current file every predetermined number of minutes. The amount of time is dependent upon the inputter's typing skills, and level of

```
Setup

     1 - Backup

     2 - Cursor Speed            30 cps

     3 - Display

     4 - Fast Save (unformatted)     No

     5 - Initial Settings

     6 - Keyboard Layout

     7 - Location of Auxiliary Files

     8 - Units of Measure
```
Fig.1-1, Setup

frustration and stress if data is lost. Ten minutes is probably a good average, but this should be less if there are power outage problems or if you are working with a clone that tends to hang, do crazy things or, in general, be a nuisance. The other type of backup is the duplication of the entire file. This is not an exact copy of the file saved today, but it is a copy of the file most recently saved. It is always one step behind, great for checking revisions and editing. This file has an extension (.BK!) .

The first automatically timed backup file goes into a *dummy* file called WP}WP{.BK1, the second into a file with the extension .BV1. If the current screen is lost, then this file can be retrieved. Sometimes a message will come on the screen to *rename* or *delete* the backup file. That means that the backup file from a previous work session is still stored in the .BV1 file. You can either save that file under a new name or delete it altogether, depending upon how secure you feel. There are those who are disconcerted by this message, because the computer will not do anything until this question is answered. After the first time that a backup file has to be used because the current file has been lost for whatever reason, this message will be greatly appreciated.

2 CURSOR SPEED (SEE SPEED, PAGE 4)

3 DISPLAY, see Fig.1-2, Setup, display

> **1 AUTOMATICALLY FORMAT AND REWRITE**
> This is very much like the recalculate command on a spreadsheet. A *yes* will cause WP to format the text on screen during the editing process. A *no* will reformat as the document is scrolled on the screen.
>
> **2 COLORS/FONTS/ATTRIBUTES**
> This screen determines only how these three areas will show up on the screen. The choices are *blink, bold, blocked, underlined, or normal.* If you are going to change these, do so in the beginning of the learning process to avoid massive confusion.
>
> **3 DISPLAY DOCUMENT COMMENTS**
> Remember the REM statements from the old days of programming in Basic, a statement which was only a

Setup: Display

1 - Automatically Format and Rewrite   Yes

2 - Colors/Fonts/Attributes

3 - Display Document Comments   Yes

4 - Filename on the Status Line   Yes

5 - Graphics Screen Type   Hercules 720x348 mono

6 - Hard Return Display Character

7 - Menu Letter Display   BOLD

8 - Side-by-side Columns Display   Yes

Fig.1-2, Setup, display

message to the author and had no effect on the program? The document comment is the same, it is a comment not printed and is shown on the screen only by the choice of the author.

4 FILENAME ON THE STATUS LINE
This displays the filename on the status line at the bottom of the screen, a great function to avoid confusion.

5 GRAPHICS SCREEN TYPE
This is automatically established by WP during the installation process; it should only be changed if more than one monitor is being used.

6 HARD RETURN DISPLAY CHARACTER
This sets the display of the hard return. If you type with the REVEAL CODES screen activated, it will probably not be necessary to change this. Otherwise, it might be

helpful to show hard returns as a bold box or as a character from the character set.

7 MENU LETTER DISPLAY
Traditionally the mnemonic menus are shown in bold. It is possible to change by size, font, or attribute.

8 SIDE-BY-SIDE COLUMNS DISPLAY
When in the column mode, the text columns will appear side by side on the screen. To facilitate editing, it is sometimes beneficial to change this option to *no*, and view the columns as continuous text until editing is complete.

4 FAST SAVE (UNFORMATTED)
This save is fast because it saves the document without formatting. But formatting must occur before printing can take place. If the cursor is moved to the end of the document (HOME, HOME, DOWN ARROW), then the document will be formatted before the save and it can be printed from the disk, a good habit to get into, especially if the user is utilizing sneaker-net to share printers.

5 INITIAL SETTINGS, see Fig.1-3, Initial settings.

1 BEEP OPTIONS
The options are beeping to occur on *error, hyphenation* and/or *search failure*. Beeps can be great helps or irritating roommates; this is a personal choice item.

2 DATE FORMAT, see Fig.1-4, Date format
This is the date that will appear when the *SHFT F5* is used. The format follows the examples exactly. If commas, spaces, slashes, or any other type of divider is to be used, it should be placed between the format codes. You even have the option of abbreviating month and day--let your creativity reign!

The date code, $^\wedge$D, will automatically insert the date during a *Merge* (SEE MERGE, SHFT F9, PAGE 65)

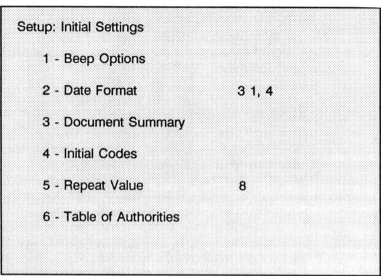

Setup: Initial Settings

   1 - Beep Options

   2 - Date Format   3 1, 4

   3 - Document Summary

   4 - Initial Codes

   5 - Repeat Value   8

   6 - Table of Authorities

Fig.1-3, Initial settings

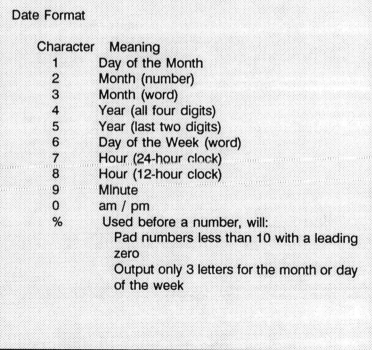

Date Format

Character	Meaning
1	Day of the Month
2	Month (number)
3	Month (word)
4	Year (all four digits)
5	Year (last two digits)
6	Day of the Week (word)
7	Hour (24-hour clock)
8	Hour (12-hour clock)
9	Minute
0	am / pm
%	Used before a number, will: Pad numbers less than 10 with a leading zero Output only 3 letters for the month or day of the week

Fig.1-4, Date format

9

3 DOCUMENT SUMMARY
This provides an automatic creation of a summary during the exit process, and it allows you to enter a subject for future searching. The *RE:* is the default; you can either change it completely or simply add the subject.

4 INITIAL CODES
This establishes default formatting codes which will become part of every document, and will be retained with the document even if the document becomes a part of another document. Some examples might be page numbering, margins, fonts, whatever the user feels are necessary to be kept with the document. These are especially useful if you transport files via floppy disk from one computer to another. The default codes ensure that the margins and the font will be the same; in other words, that the document will not have to be reformatted because of a change in machinery.

5 REPEAT VALUE
This is a repetition feature: any character can be repeated a designated number of times by striking the ESC key, the number of required repetitions, and the character.

6 TABLE OF AUTHORITIES
A standard table of authorities has the following format:
dot leader..............flush right page number
underline codes are maintained
double spacing is used between *authorities*
It is possible to create the opposite of any of these three by changing the default from no to yes, or vice versa.

6 KEYBOARD LAYOUT

A keyboard with an F11 and an F12 key is considered an enhanced keyboard. If you have one, select this option; if you do not, consider purchasing one. The F11 key becomes *REVEAL CODES*, and the F12 becomes *BLOCK*. Additional macros are also associated with this keyboard choice.

The standard keyboard can be used as is, or the function keys can be recoded to reflect different functions. For instance, some might feel more comfortable if the *F1* key were the help key instead of the *F3*. It is possible to edit the key definitions by selecting the *key edit* screen.

7 LOCATION OF AUXILIARY FILES

Auxiliary files are the dictionary and thesaurus files either originally packaged with WP, or the supplemental ones created by the user. Backup files, hyphenation files, macros, printer files, and style library files also fall within this category. Storing these files in a specific directory other than the directory in which text files are stored makes the maintenance and housekeeping of the hard disk much easier. Isolation in another directory also prevents accidental erasure. This option is highly beneficial and is strongly recommended.

8 UNITS OF MEASURE

The chosen units of measure show up on the status line at the bottom of the screen. Because of the variety of fonts and point sizes available, it is optimal to use inches even though WP 4.2 fanatics will prefer lines, (units). It is also possible to select centimeters or points. To make life wonderfully easy it is possible to select inches, yet enter the information in centimeters. WP automatically doing the conversion.

TIP -- SHFT F1   If WP seems to be acting up uncontrollably, much like a two-year old child, check this screen. You may be expecting a certain default action which inadvertently has been changed to reflect an entirely different action.

CTRL F1   This is the gateway to the DOS environment, also known as the Shell. While in the *Shell*, it is possible to execute DOS commands or, if there is enough memory, to actually run other programs. For an average machine of 640K RAM, however, it will probably not be possible to run many other programs because WP 5.0 takes up so much room. The Shell is useful to get directory information quickly, to set the clock, or do other basic maintenance. When all actions are completed, type *EXIT* to return to the program. The screen display will reflect the current file intact. Quite frankly, this was much more useful in WP 4.2 because of available memory. Not only has WP increased in size, but other programs such as Procomm, which has become ProCommPlus, have also increased in size preventing running of telecommunications from the WP Shell. All this leads to the obvious: consider purchasing up to at least 1.2 MB RAM.

ALT F1 The WP THESAURUS is a most useful feature. It is not nearly as complete or complex as Roget's, but it certainly serves equally well in most cases. It is possible to search for synonyms for the word on which the cursor currently resides, or to look up any word. Use the *1* Replace Word command to completely replace, without any retyping, the old for the new. The words with alpha characters preceding them can be expanded by simply typing that letter. It is not always necessary to chose the most basic grammatical structure to *hit;* WP quite successfully determines the base word, and gives an appropriate list of synonyms, verbs, and antonyms. To get from one column to the next, just use the right and left arrow keys. If you haven't used this yet, DO SO!!

F2

F2 *SEARCH*es for a word, phrase, or code. As with other commands, this one is affected by the location of the cursor within the document. An **F2** will search forward from the cursor; a **SHFT-F2** will search backward. Type the word to be searched at the colon; but do not press return, or the search will include a search for a return code also. Either **F2** or **ESC** will initiate the search. After the first word is found, the search is continued by pressing **F2, F2**. Finally to return to the spot where the search was initiated, press **CTRL HOME, CTRL HOME.**

TIP -- F2 To search for a word that is also part of other words, place a space before, after, and/or before and/or after the word.

To search for *uppercase*, use uppercase. Lowercase search requests find both uppercase and lowercase matches.

The wildcard character is **CTRL V, CTRL X.** Do not use it as the first character, and do not use with codes.

To include footers, headers, graphics and text boxes, end and footnotes, use **HOME, F2.**

SHFT F2 reverses the **F2** Search procedure.

CTRL F2 *SPELL* checks, one of the greatest features on WP. The options are to check the spelling of a word, all of the words on the page on which the cursor presently resides, or all of the words within the document. It is also possible to look up a particular word, to count how many words are in the document, and to use, in addition to WP's dictionary, a supplemental dictionary created by you to include words idiosyncratic to your experiences. When WP finds a word that is not within the dictionary, choices are displayed on the screen which are possible substitutes. The misspelled word can be replaced by typing the alpha letter preceding the correctly spelled word. Sometimes, the word is simply not in the dictionary. At that point, use **4 Edit** to either edit completely, or try to get closer to the correct form. In the edit mode, the right and left arrows, backspace, and delete keys will function. If the revised word is not found within the dictionary, WP will highlight it again before going on. If the word is not in the dictionary, you can either add it to the supplemental dictionary, or skip it. The supplemental dictionary can be edited as a WP file; if a word is added by mistake it can be revised. During the skip process, if you choose *skip*, WP will skip that letter combination every time it occurs during this spell check. If you want it skipped only once, then choose the only once option. WP also stops when words occur twice in succession; the options for correction are delete one of the occurrences, or skip. Whenever a number is part of a word (*10th*, for example), WP will consider that it is an incorrect spelling. When looking up words, a **?** will act as a wildcard for one letter, and a ***** will act as zero to many letters. WP will also match words on the sound if a spelling match is not possible.

If a word has been spelled consistently, but incorrectly, throughout the entire document, spell check will correct the first error, as well as all subsequent incorrect spellings. WP actually learns how the user misspells. If a word, such as library, is frequently misspelled, WP will *remember* that misspelling, and offer the correct spelling first. There is a certain amount of efficiency built in.

The count simply provides a count of how many words are in the document. This is great for an article assignment for which one is paid by the word, or for laying out newsletters when you have an idea of about how many words fill a column. It is also very satisfying to check every once in a while to see how many words you have written, one of the intrinsic rewards of using WP.

SOME SAMPLE SPELL CHECKS TO TRY:
    LIB?R*
    LIBR*
    LIB*R*
Please note: spell checking does not eliminate the need for human proofreading!

ALT F2   *SEARCH AND REPLACE* not only searches, but also replaces. For the searching process, the technique is exactly the same as the **F2** function. there is an initial option *w/confirm?* which allows the user to okay the replace command with each hit. Unless the search item is unique, this should probable be *yes.* The second step *Search,* is then followed by *Replace* which follows the same rules until, finally, an **F2** to start the process. This is great for searching for a period followed by double spaces, which creates white rivers in a kerned document, and replacing it with a period followed by one space at the end of a sentence. It is useful for global replacement of acronyms with the fully written phrase. It is great for replacing abbreviations with the word. All tabs can be replaced with indents. You can even search for a word or phrase and replace it with nothing. You can replace all *normalized* versions of the name of your library with a bolded, underlined version.

TIP -- ALT F2   Do not use the enter key unless you want it included in the Search and Replace procedure. For instance, you may want to replace all instances of two hard returns with one hard return.

If you are a poor typist and consistently type *form* instead of *from* use search and replace with confirm to look for all those *form's,* which will be ignored by the spell checker because in fact they are spelled correctly, even though they are used improperly.

If you have consistently typed a word with an initial lowercase letter which should have been

15

uppercase, a search and replace will correct the problem.

After a merge, a search and replace will remove page breaks between records. (SEE MERGE, SHFT F9, PAGE 65.)

F3

F3 brings up the Help screens. Help will be provided for any area in WP by typing the function keys with their appropriate auxiliary key, or by typing the first letter of the action, for instance, **b** for *block*. Striking **F3** twice brings up the template for keyboards with function keys on the left. To exit any help screen, strike the **ENTER** or the **SPACE BAR**, all other keys will just give you more help. It is possible to go from one help screen to another by typing in the function keys. These screens are quite detailed, and will often preclude the use of a manual.

SHFT F3 switches to the second document screen. The second screen can be used exactly as the first. Having two documents available at the same time is especially useful when copying blocks of text from one document to another. (SEE BLOCK, ALT F4, PAGE 22) It is helpful if you are working on a main, lengthy document but need to look quickly at and possibly revise or print another document. We all know that days are never completely interrupt-free; using the two screens eases some of the frustrations of interruptions. Again, if you are working with a machine in the lower ranges of megahertzes, in other words, slower than molasses, this saves time because it is not necessary to save, exit, load, save, exit, reload the first document again. When doing a major print job, it is possible to initiate the job and clear the screen, but how many times have you done this and then had a print problem of some kind, had to reload the document, and do a complete or partial print again? Another use is to load a file with a page format that you want to repeat, block the codes, and copy them to the second document. If you are working on one document and suddenly have an idea about another, it is very easy to switch screens, load the second, revise, and exit.

CTRL F3 gives three options: **0** Rewrite; **1** Window; **2** Line Draw

0 REWRITE relates to **SHFT F1, 3 (D), 1 (A).** If you have selected to turn the automatic format feature off,

17

then it is possible to reformat a screen any time during the writing or editing process by selecting either **0 (R) or CTRL F3, CTRL F3.**

1 WINDOW relates to **SHFT F3.** The window is the screen which contains the document, a full screen window being 24 lines. If you want both the first and second documents to appear on the same screen, reduce the size of the window. For two documents, the number of lines would usually be 12. To get from one screen to the other, just use **SHFT F3** to go back and forth. To eliminate the window or split screen, just reverse the process. if you are using the reveal codes feature extensively, you may prefer to look at each document on its own screen.

2 LINE DRAW is not really a paint software type feature, but it does allow limited drawing of lines to create boxes, borders, and graphs either on a blank screen or around existing text.

1 | draws a single line
2 ‖ draws a double line
3 * draws a line made up of asterisks
4 Change allows you to change that third option to a variety of lines of different thicknesses and appearances,
5 Erase erases lines as the cursor is moved over them. Use this with caution, it also erases text.
6 Move moves the cursor without actually having an effect on the lines which have been drawn.

ALT F3 is the *REVEAL CODES* feature and is probably the most important feature for successful use of WP. Every WP special feature is represented by a code that is not visible on the screen. *REVEAL CODES* shows all the codes and exactly where they are so that it is apparent which text is affected. One of the problems that users seem to have with WP is the repetition of codes. For instance, a margin set will be established. Later the user will go back and insert another margin set. Both margin sets will affect the document. Unless the user intended to actually maintain two different margins, it is necessary to delete the unwanted codes. This type of code, as with most others, can be deleted only in the **REVEAL CODES** mode. Although the reveal codes screen will be askew because the codes force text to line up in unfamiliar ways, it is a very good practice to work with this screen on most of the time.

TIP ALT F3 When using a paired code, that is, one which has a beginning and ending such as, [BOLD][bold], it is not necessary to retype **F6** to end the code, or as in the case of italics, small caps, etc., to *normalize* the text; it is only necessary to use the right arrow to move the cursor past the end of the code pair.

When deleting characters within a paired code, put the cursor on the characters to make sure the codes themselves are not deleted. If you want the characters to be moved outside of the code pair, move the cursor to the extreme right of left of the pair, and use **F1** to restore the characters.

Use the Block feature to move codes by cursoring to the beginning of the codes and blocking codes and/or text. The Copy and Move feature will also work for blocks of codes. (SEE BLOCK, ALT F4, PAGE 22)

F4

F4

indents a line the same number of spaces that a tab does, except that using **F4** also indents all the following lines until a HARD RETURN is used. To create what is commonly known as a hanging paragraph (this is when the first line of the paragraph is at the regular left margin but all of the rest of the paragraph is indented), use **F4, SHFT TAB.**

SHFT F4

will indent the paragraph from both margins. This is great for long quotations, (especially if you add an extra flair with italics or text of a smaller point size).

CTRL F4

is the cut and paste feature for which word processors are so famous. These are four options:

>**1** Sentence - allows you to work with an entire sentence.
>**2** Paragraph - allows you to work with an entire paragraph.
>**3** Page - allows you to work with an entire page.
>**4** Retrieve - brings back the text that you are working with from the three choices above; or retrieves text which was most recently blocked. This second feature is a super way of copying. For instance, if you were creating a petition for patrons to sign to urge legislators to increase library funding, at the beginning of the codes for the line you might create a horizontal line, then use **CTRL F4, 1 (S), 4 (R)** repeatedly until the entire page is filled with lines.

Within **4** Retrieve, text is described by areas which are defined as:

1 Block - a section of text, more or less than one sentence, paragraph, or page.

2 Tabular Column - not a newspaper or parallel column, but a column of numbers of text with tabs, indents, hard returns as opposed to the columnar controls.

3 Rectangle - may just be all of the text between the margins, just a piece of it, in the shape of a rectangle. Use with **Block, ALT F4.**

After choosing a block of text with which to work, the next options are:

1 Move - actually moves the text from its current position to be placed somewhere else.

2 Copy - does not remove the text from its position, but does make a copy of that text to be placed anywhere else.

3 Delete - removes the text completely, but it can be retrieved with the F1 restore feature.

4 Append - will add the text, but not graphics, under consideration to the end of another file.

ALT F4 known as *BLOCK*, highlights or *blocks* the text that is to be altered in some way, by moving or changing the attributes or font or style. Use this by placing the cursor at the beginning of the text to be altered, press **ALT F4**, move the cursor to the end of the block, and then use either **CTRL F4** to move or copy, or **CTRL F8** to change an attribute, or a text formatting command such as center or flush right. It is also possible to save or print the block, delete the block, mark it as part of an index, sort the text within, or to spell check just that section of text. Actually you should assume that you can do just about anything to a block until it doesn't work.

When in the block mode, a **RETURN** will copy the whole line unless it is the very last line in the document, in

22

which case you will have to cursor to the end. An easier method is to turn the block on, type a character, either a period for the end of a sentence or a character, and the block will go to that next period or character.

F5

lists the files within a directory. the default directory is WP50, which is the directory created during the installation process. you can either change the directory after striking the **F5** key once, or strike it twice and go directly to the default directory.

It is possible to maintain files and directories from within the **F5** function. A directory listing might look like Fig.5-1, Directory listing.

The screen can be explained as follows, from left to right, starting at the top left:

- current date
- time
- definition of the current directory

second line

- the size of the document currently loaded
- the number of free bytes on the entire hard disk
- how many bytes on the hard disk have been used in toto

```
03/16/90  16:52          Directory D:\WP50\*.*
Document size: 0 Free: 4063232 Used: 5820673 Files:  383

. <CURRENT>   <DIR>              .. <PARENT>    <DIR>
SHELL.      <DIR>   02/18/00 13:39   2PS.      2213 05/22/89 23:20
8514A.WPD    3476  09/16/88 15:57   89RA.      5946 07/23/89 23:18
8PT2.        7830  01/01/80 00:56   90RA.     16038 08/21/89 23:29
9PT2.       10651  01/01/80 00:08   ACQ.      10182 09/20/89 21:49
ACQ.SF       517   09/20/89 21:52   ADDGLIMM.  1922   05/08/89
01:09 AIDS.  22753  10/07/88 14:30   AIDSBIB.  1793 01/09/89 12:02
AIRPLANE.WPG  8484  09/16/88 15:57   ALBOOK. 179151 02/11/90 05:24




1 Retrieve; 2 Delete; 3 Move/Rename; 4 Print; 5 Text In;
6 Look; 7 Other Directory; 8 Copy; 9 Word Search; N Name Search:6
```

Fig.5-1, Directory listing

• the number of files within this directory.

Files with <DIR> following the name are actually directories, the parent is the root directory.

File names are sometimes followed by a period and a three letter extension which can usually be guessed. The basic extensions are as follows:

.wpm   WordPerfect macro
.prs   printer definition file
.wpg   WordPerfect graphic
.com   command file (DOS)
.exe   execute file (DOS)
.bk!   WordPerfect backup file
.   text file

The files are followed by the size in bytes and the date and time of the last save.
The cursor and page keys work to move the cursor. Whatever file is being considered is highlighted

The options on this menu are:

1 Retrieve will load a file onto the screen. If a file is already loaded it will place the new file exactly where the cursor is located, but you will be offered the option of continuing before that happens.

2 Delete will remove the highlighted file from existence, again a second chance will be offered.

3 Move/Rename will either rename or relocate the file.

4 Print sends the file to the printer without retrieving.

5 Text in retrieves a file that has been saved in ASCII format. Files that have been downloaded from electronic mail or online services are often in ASCII format. Although they can sometimes be loaded as if they were regular files, retrieving them as ASCII files will probably create less havoc with margins and formatting.

6 Look is one of the handiest commands on this menu. It allows you to look at a file without actually retrieving it. You cannot perform any action on the file other than scrolling through the pages. It is helpful when you cannot remember what file name has been used, to check where you started or left off, or just to make sure this is really the file you want to print.

7 Other directory will either create a new directory or will cause a different directory to be listed. It is better to use the parent <DIR> selection to get to another directory. If you are going to the A: drive you will have to use the other directory command, but then you will be in the a: drive, which is slower and which will insist that there be a disk present, etc.

8 Copy makes a duplicate file in another file or directory. If you copy in the same directory to a file that is new but which has the same name as an existent file, the existent file will be replaced but, as usual, you will be given a chance to back out.

9 Word search is an incredible feature that may serve as a substitute for Norton's Utilities. It allows you to search all or only specifically marked files for a word or phrase. Within this are the following search options:

> **1** Doc Summary searches the summary only.
> **2** First Page searches the first page or first 4,000 characters.
> **3** Entire Doc searches through the entire document.
> **4** Conditions more precisely defines the search. You might consider that you are creating a search strategy with *and* conditions using this feature. See Fig.5-2, Word search. All parameters that are established within this menu will be satisfied by the search.

The first four options are exactly what they appear to be. Dates do not have to be exact, but do need to include

Word Search

   1 - Perform Search on   All 209 File(s)

   2 - Undo Last Search

   3 - Reset Search Conditions

   4 - File Date   No
      From (MM/DD/YY):   (All)
      To   (MM/DD/YY):   (All)

                Word Pattern(s)

   5 - First Page
   6 - Entire Doc
   7 - Document Summary
      Creation Date (e.g. Nov)
      Descriptive Name
      Subject/Account
      Author
      Typist
      Comments

Fig.5-2, Word search

at least two //'s and the day, month, or year within the appropriate slash area, that is, the month goes before the first slash, etc.

The word patterns are able to utilize the ? and * as in the *F2* function. To search a phrase, enclose the words within quotation marks. The search does not distinguish between upper-case and lower-case letters. It is also possible to integrate more sophisticated Boolean logic within this function:

        a semicolon or space   = AND
        a comma   = OR

28

These two can be combined with each other or with quotation marks to create complicated search strategies, just as if you were using Dialog. (This might be a good way to introduce students to developing search strategies before going online.)

N Name Search searches within the file names listed on the directory. It allows you to search for the first character of a file name, any number of additional characters, or the entire name. This is very similar to the browse mode of an automated public access catalog or a catalog on CD-ROM.

TIP -- F5 use the asterisk to mark files to perform a multiple copy, print, move, or delete. To remove the mark just type another asterisk which will cancel the first.

SHFT F5 establishes dates and outlines. The options are as follows:

1 Date Text inserts the computer's current date into the text. This works great if your computer clock is right.

2 Date Code inserts the code for the date so that the date will always be current, regardless of when the document is created and when it is printed.

3 Date Format establishes just how the date will look. See Fig.1-4, Date format.

4 Outline **[Par Num:Auto]** turns on the outline feature, which is defined by **6 Define.**

5 Para Num **[Par Num:Auto]**numbers one paragraph at a time as opposed to an outline which *numbers* every line. Both the outline and paragraph number feature depend upon the definition.

6 Define establishes the numbering system and levels for the paragraph or outline style. See Fig.5-3, Paragraph numbering.

Although this looks overwhelming, it is simply a matter of choosing which format you prefer, or defining your own style, and then using it.

TIP -- SHFT F5   Remember to re-establish the definition every time you want to change a paragraph/outline style in the document; the style will be effective after the point of definition, which is wherever the cursor was.

The numbering system will automatically correct itself if paragraphs or lines are inserted or deleted anywhere within the area in which the

---

Paragraph Number Definition

1 - Starting Paragraph Number   1
    (in legal style)

		Levels					
	1	2	3	4	5	6	7	8
2 - Paragraph	1.	a.	i.	(1)	(a)	(i)	1)	a)
3 - Outline	I.	A.	1.	a.	(1)	(a)	i)	a)
4 - Legal (1.1.1)	1	.1	.1	.1	.1	*.1	.1	.1
5 - Bullets	^G -	•	*	+	•	x		
6 - User-defined								

Current Definition   2 .1 .1 .1

Number Style	Punctuation
1 - Digits	# - No punctuation
A - Upper case letters	#. - Trailing period
a - Lower case letters	#) - Trailing parenthesis
I - Upper case roman	(#) - Enclosing parentheses
i - Lower case roman	.# - All levels separated by
	period
Other character - Bullet	(e.g. 2.1.3.4)

Fig.5-3, Paragraph numbering

outline feature has been turned on. This makes editing an outline incredibly easy, and should make kids want to write papers.

It is possible to restart numbering at any point by using the Starting Paragraph Number option, and just typing whatever new number you want to start with. For instance, you might want each chapter within a document to start with the chapter number.

CTRL F5 provides alternative methods to save or to retrieve files that were not originally created in WP 5.0.

1 DOS Text is a text that has the basic code information for returns, tabs, spaces, and text, but does not contain formatting codes. This is the format that is usually most successful in electronic mail transfer. The options are to save in DOS format or to retrieve a file that is in DOS. You will probably have to experiment with the two types of retrieve to find which best suits your document. The *CR/LF to [SRt]* does not create an abundance of hard returns and probably should be tried first.

2 Password locks a document so that no one else can access or print the file without the secret password. You have two chances to enter the password, but if you forget it, you will have no chances for retrieval. It is possible to unlock the document by removing the password after a document has been retrieved. This should be used with caution; but it is great for confidential personnel files, contract negotiation documents, the pornographic novel you are writing during coffee breaks, and other potentially controversial work occupying your time.

3 Save Generic saves a file with some text formatting codes so that most word processors will be able to retrieve the file. You should not have to do major editing to maintain a semblance of the document as you see it.

31

4 Save WP 4.2 saves the file as if it had been created in WP 4.2. Most documents in WP 4.2 are retrievable in WP 5.0, but it is not possible to reverse the process. The main reason for using this save format is to save a file that will be used in a program like Ventura which has not been updated to receive WP 5.0 files. Presently, a WP 5.0 file in Ventura will hang the program, without relief, although supposedly the new version of Ventura will correct this problem but only for holders of the new version.

5 Comment relates to the setup (**F1**). Comments are statements to or by the author, but which do not necessarily appear on the screen, and definitely do not appear on the print version. This can be used like a notebook file, or a yellow sticky; and then, later, if desired, the comment can be transformed into text and become part of the actual document.

ALT F5 marks the text for automatic references, tables of contents, and indexes. The options are as follows:

1 Auto Ref is very much like the *see also* references in the card catalog. It is possible to mark a reference and then, within the document, to create a see reference which refers to the correct page number, figure number, or footnote number, of the marked reference. As with other numbered features in WP, this will automatically update and correct numbers if there are changes after the initial creation.

2 Subdoc is a piece of a master document. The master document is the skeleton of the whole. It might comprise the table of contents, the subdocs, and the index. Creating a subdoc actually inserts a code that refers to the complete subdoc file which, during expansion of the master document, will be loaded in its totality.

3 Index marks the text, words, or phrase that will become the index. It is possible either to mark text as you type, or to block text and mark for indexing during the edit process. For a long and complicated index, it is also possible to create a concordance, in which case it is not necessary to mark text. The concordance index is *easier* than marking, but it is dependent upon the availability and amount of RAM.

4 ToA Short Form is the table of authorities for a legal brief. The short form is the *ibid* for citations of cases, statues, rules and regulations which already have been cited in full form.

5 Define establishes the levels of tables of contents, indexes, lists, and table of authorities.

6 Generate actually creates the table of contents, etc. It also expands and condenses master documents, compares documents, and removes or inserts redlines and strikeouts.

F6

F6   creates bolded text.

SHFT F6   centers text on the page.

CTRL F6   lines up text or numbers on the chosen default character. The WP default is the *period,* but you might want to choose a space to line up text vertically for a list. As with other format codes, whatever follows the code will be affected until the code is changed again. Using this command causes the cursor to go to the next tab and move text to the left until the *tab align default, **CTRL F6, TAB,*** or ***ENTER*** is struck.

with	without
12.34	12.23
234.56	234.23
234556.77	23345677.88

(Notice that the *h* in *with* lines up as if it had a decimal place following the letter. This would be useful for typing call numbers if you wanted all the levels to be lined up.)

ALT F6   moves the text to line up flush right with the right margin. This command will work after the fact by going to the beginning of the line in question and entering the command. If you wanted to move lots of lines to the right, it is more efficient, but not necessary, to block the text.

F7

F7   saves a document and exits the program. There is an opportunity to replace an existing document of the same name with the current document, which is sometimes useful if you have used that filename but didn't remember. You also have the opportunity to exit WP. If you choose not to leave, then essentially what you have done is clear the screen so that you can begin work on a new document. If you decide that you don't really want to clear the screen after the save, press **F1** to cancel the clear screen function; the current document will remain on the screen. If you frequently save your document because of a potential hardware problem, it is more efficient to use the **F10** save function. (SEE SAVE, F10, PAGE 75.)

SHFT F7   prints the page. See Fig.7-1, Print menu.

1 FULL DOCUMENT Prints the complete document, all pages in order.

2 PAGE Prints the page on which the cursor is currently residing.

3 DOCUMENT ON DISK Prints documents which have been previously saved to disk. It is possible to print all or selected pages of the document.

4 CONTROL PRINTER, see Fig.7-2, Printer control screen. The current job is the one that is being printed by WP, not necessarily by the printer. In other words, it is the job that WP is sending to the printer at this time. After the print jobs have been dumped into the printer's memory, WP no longer has control, and will indicate on this screen that the print job is done, although the pages may not yet have appeared. The jobs are queued in the order in which the print job is requested. This is completely chronological. Again, the status is WP's status. If it is printing, it is sending a formatted page to the printer. It also notes here if it is downloading fonts. (SEE FONTS, CTRL F8, PAGE 62.) The paper and location are only of importance if there is an extra paper tray and bins or feeders. The message line lets you know if any problems have been encountered and, if so, what steps you

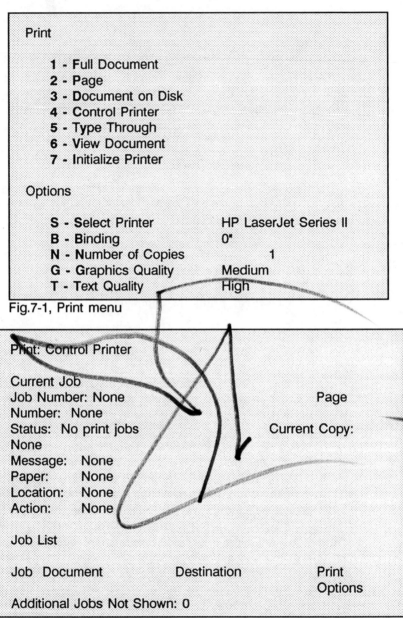

Print

    1 - Full Document
    2 - Page
    3 - Document on Disk
    4 - Control Printer
    5 - Type Through
    6 - View Document
    7 - Initialize Printer

Options

    S - Select Printer   HP LaserJet Series II
    B - Binding   0"
    N - Number of Copies   1
    G - Graphics Quality   Medium
    T - Text Quality   High

Fig.7-1, Print menu

Print: Control Printer

Current Job
Job Number: None   Page
Number: None
Status: No print jobs   Current Copy:
None
Message: None
Paper: None
Location: None
Action: None

Job List

Job Document   Destination   Print
                                          Options
Additional Jobs Not Shown: 0

Fig.7-2, Printer control screen

should take to relieve the situation. The job list reflects the top three items in the queue. The destination is the printer port, and the print options tells what kind of paper type you have set up for that particular printer on that particular printer port. If there are more than three jobs lined up in the queue, the *additional jobs* will tell you how many. At the end of this screen are commands that more definitively control the printing process:

1 Cancel - Cancels any job or all jobs, the choice will be given to you upon implementation of this command.

2 Rush - In a society of instant gratification, when the library director wants that acquisitions list now, and it is tenth in the queue, this will allow you to move it ahead of other print jobs.

3 Display - Shows a list of all the print jobs waiting patiently in the queue.

4 Go - Restarts the printer if it has been stopped for any reason. This will also come up if you have used a manual paper feed command.

5 Stop - Doesn't actually cancel a job, but stops the printer so that you can fix the ribbon, change paper, or take a coffee break.

5 TYPE THROUGH This feature allows you to return to the Dark Ages and use the printer as if it were a typewriter. The option is to print one character at a time or an entire line at a time. The printing occurs exactly where the printhead is located at the time the **ENTER** key is stricken. There is limited control of the printer with the use of printer commands.

6 VIEW DOCUMENT This is the greatest feature that has been added to the 5.0 version. With the presence of an installed graphics card, it allows the user to actually see what the page layout will look like without printing the page. It saves time, paper, and frustration. There are four options: to look at a full page (reduced); to look at the page at its true size -- 100%; to look at it at double its real size -- 200%; or to look at two pages which face each other. This last is great for inside pages of newsletters. During the actual typing and layout, it is typical to think of every page as a right page, because that is what you are working on on the screen. With the view, facing pages feature, the two pages are seen as they will be in the final printed document; layout errors leap off the page and can be corrected or revised before the actual printing. If the microcomputer is 4 mhz, this process will be s l o w; with a machine of 10 mhz or greater, the process becomes bearable. If you are going to use view often, it is recommended that the timed backup be set at five to ten minutes. Sometimes, for whatever reason, view will cause a machine to hang, especially a clone. Make sure your work is saved before you look at it in all its magnificence!

Please note that the viewing will not show you *exactly* what the page will look like when printed, but it will be very close. For instance, italics may appear as underline. Finally it is not necessary to wait until a full screen appears before changing the command, if you really want to see 100% and it is set on full page, strike 1 while the full page is scrolling down. It saves time and the program doesn't mind.

7 INITIALIZE PRINTER If soft fonts, as opposed to cartridge type fonts, are marked to be downloaded, this command will initiate the download process. It is only necessary to do this once, unless the printers are turned off or some kind of catastrophic occurrence takes place.

S SELECT PRINTER The printer on this line is the printer that you have selected as your default printer. The document will be formatted specifically for this printer. For further control of this process, use 3 Edit within this menu. See Fig.7-3, Printer selection.

> 1 NAME is the name of the printer file for the printer currently selected.

> 2 PORT is the serial or parallel port to which that particular printer is connected.

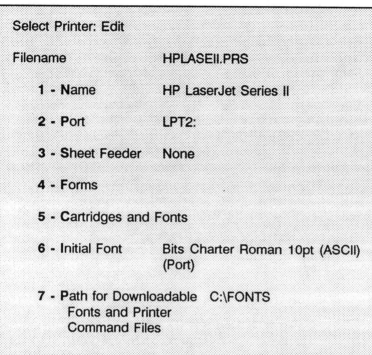

Select Printer: Edit

Filename HPLASEII.PRS

1 - Name HP LaserJet Series II

2 - Port LPT2:

3 - Sheet Feeder None

4 - Forms

5 - Cartridges and Fonts

6 - Initial Font Bits Charter Roman 10pt (ASCII) (Port)

7 - Path for Downloadable C:\FONTS Fonts and Printer Command Files

Fig.7-3, Printer selection

3 SHEET FEEDER indicates the presence of a sheet feeder.

4 FORMS changes the size of the paper. See Fig.7-4, Printer forms.

Form type is the name of the form to be used. Size is the actual dimensions of the paper. Orientation refers to landscape or portrait mode. If the form is initially present, WP will not stop during the print job for manual placement of the form in the printer. Location is for printers with bin options. Offset refers to the loading of paper and where the printhead actually starts printing. Delete removes the currently highlighted form definition. Edit allows revision of a form definition. The most commonly used of the optional forms will be legal size and envelope.

```
Select Printer: Forms
                          Orient Init      Offset
    Form type       Size   P L Pres Location  Top Side

    Envelope      4" x 9.5"    N Y Y    Manual  0"     0"
    Standard      8.5" x 11"   Y Y Y    Contin  0"     0"
    [ALL OTHERS]  Width ≤ 8.5"  N        Manual  0"     0"

    If the requested form is not available, then printing stops
    and WordPerfect waits for a form to be inserted in the ALL
    OTHERS location. If the requested form is larger than the
    ALL OTHERS form, the width is set to the maximum width.
```

Fig.7-4, Printer forms

5 CARTRIDGES AND FONTS is the list of all possible choices of soft fonts or cartridge fonts. (SEE FONTS, CTRL F8, PAGE 62.)

6 INITIAL FONT, again, is the default font choice for this printer. All attributes are based on this font. (SEE FONTS, CTRL F8, PAGE 62.)

7 PATH FOR DOWNLOADABLE FONTS AND PRINTER COMMAND FILES tells WP where to go when looking for a font or printer file. It is really useful to store font files and printer files in a separate directory or subdirectory. It is very confusing if these files are intermingled with all the text files.

B BINDING If the document will be bound, this command will shift the text as necessary for odd and even pages to give an extra margin for binding. The command will not be imbedded within the document, and so will have to be selected with every print job. If the binding width is changed with one print job, it will affect all other print jobs until it is changed back.

N NUMBER OF COPIES The number of copies of a document to be printed.

G GRAPHICS QUALITY Graphics can be printed in draft, medium, or high quality, or not at all. This is useful when working on drafts to save the printhead, or laser printer toner. Some printers will not print in high quality if the printer memory is limited. But, remember, the higher the quality, the better resolution the print job will have. This is especially important if the document is to be copied later on a copier or at the print shop. In some cases it may be necessary to print text without graphics, and then reverse the process, if the printer is not capable of doing both. If this is the case, it will be prudent to consider purchasing another printer--write a grant!

T TEXT QUALITY This is exactly the same as the Graphics Quality feature, except that it is the text.

CTRL F7   creates endnotes and footnotes. The options are:

1 Footnote and 2 Endnote create, edit, give a new number, or establish the definition parameters for footnotes and endnotes. Creating a note is exactly like creating a footer or header. This would have been a super feature if not for the implementation of the parenthetical citation format.

3 Endnote Placement inserts a code that will tell WP to create the endnotes at that particular place. At the time of inserting the code, WP does not yet know how much space will be needed, space will be determined by the generation of the notes. The generation will include all notes from the beginning of the text up to the point of the placement code.

Within each note function there are options. Footnote and endnote options are described below. See Fig.7-5, Note options.

Footnote Options

1 - Spacing Within Footnotes   1
              Between Footnotes   0.16"

2 - Amount of Note to Keep Together   0.5"

3 - Style for Number in Text [SUPRSCPT][Note Num][suprscpt]

4 - Style for Number in Note [SUPRSCPT][Note Num][suprscpt]

5 - Footnote Numbering Method Numbers

6 - Start Footnote Numbers each Page   No

7 - Line Separating Text and Footnotes   2-inch Line

8 - Print Continued Message   No

9 - Footnotes at Bottom of Page   Yes

Fig.7-5, Note options

Many of these are like the formatting options for a page. As has been the practice throughtout this book, the two possible keys, alpha or numeric, to select these options are given in bold.

1 - S the number of spaces between lines of text, (these can be decimals) and the number of lines between each complete footnote

2 - A if the notes need to be separated because of too many lines, how many lines minimally to keep together

3 - T   the way that the note number will look within the document, the default being superscript

4 - N   the way that the number will look in the note itself, again, the default is superscript

5 - M   the characters or letters that will be used for notes

6 - P   whether the numbering system will start again with each new page

7 - L   whether a line will be drawn to separate the text and the notes on the page

8 - C   if a note has to be split, whether a *continued* message should be printed

9 - B   where the footnotes will be placed on the page if the text does not fill up the page, otherwise the notes could appear at the immediate end of the text wherever that might be on the page

ALT F7   creates math columns and text columns.

1 Math On turns the math feature   *on* after the definition has been established.

2 Math Def (see Fig.7-6, Math column definition) sets the parameters for using math functions. Within a document it is possible to combine text and numerical columns and to perform math functions upon the numbers. The math definition option distinguishes between alpha and numeric columns, and determines whether the calculation is to occur across the row or down the columns.

3 Column On/Off turns columns on or off.

4 Column Def (see Fig.7-7, Text column definition) establishes the parameters for text columns, for which

45

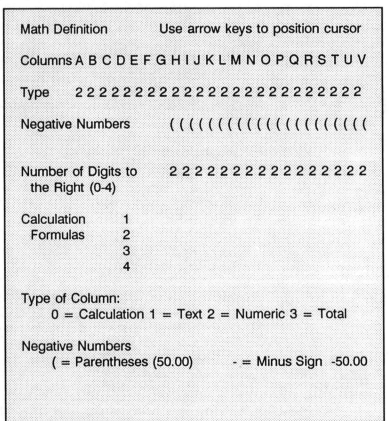

Fig.7-6, Math column definition

Parallel columns are of a horizontal perspective. These columns go across the page with the segments of information, each segment covering however many lines are needed, then the next segment repeating.

As long as the margins for the page are set before the column is defined the definition process is very simple: decide what kind of column, how many, what space between each one, and whether it must be equal for all. The columns margins will be based on the above information and will be set automatically by WP. Of course, if you are moved by creativity or perversity, it is possible to create your own column margins.

The columns margins will be based on the above information and will be set automatically by WP. Of course, if you are moved by creativity or perversity, it is possible to create your own column margins.

Text Column Definition

1 - Type   Newspaper

2 - Number of Columns   2

3 - Distance Between Columns

4 - Margins

Column	Left	Right	Column	Left	Right
1:	1"	4"	13:		
2:	4.5"	7.5"	14:		
3:			15:		
4:			16:		

Fig.7-7, Text column definition

F8

F8   underlines text.

SHFT F8   formats the page. See Fig.8-1, Format.

> 1 - Line, see Fig.8-2, Line Format. The words in brackets are the codes that will appear when Reveal Codes, ALT F3, is used.

Format

    1 - Line
Hyphenation   Line Spacing
Justification   Margins Left/Right
Line Height   Tab Set
Line Numbering   Widow/Orphan Protection

    2 - Page
Center Page (top to bottom)   New Page Number
Force Odd/Even Page   Page Numbering
Headers and Footers   Paper Size/Type
Margins Top/Bottom   Suppress

    3 - Document
Display Pitch   Redline Method
Initial Codes/Font   Summary

    4 - Other
Advance   Overstrike
Conditional End of Page   Printer Functions
Decimal Characters   Underline Spaces/Tabs
Language

Fig.8-1, Format

1 HYPHENATION   [Hyph]

The *default* setting is no hyphenation. WP follows the rules exactly when hyphenating. Unfortunately the English language does not. *Auto hyphenation* is not highly recommended. Words will be divided between two consonants regardless of what your English teacher said about those words. *Manual hyphenation* gives the option of confirming each hyphenation as it occurs. A message will appear to position the hyphen, when satisfied press the **ESC** key. An **F1** will send the word to the next line with no hyphenation.

Do not insert a hyphen during the input process, for if the document shifts during formatting the hyphen will remain and

Format: Line

1 - Hyphenation		Off
2 - Hyphenation Zone -	Left	10%
	Right	4%
3 - Justification	Yes	
4 - Line Height	Auto	
5 - Line Numbering	No	
6 - Line Spacing	1	
7 - Margins - Left	2.06"	
	Right	2.06"
8 - Tab Set	0", every 0.5"	
9 - Widow/Orphan Protection	No	

Fig.8-2, Line format

cause problems. If the hyphenation process is used, all hyphens created (soft hyphens according to WP) will disappear if they are no longer necessary. A soft hyphen can be created by the **CTRL, hyphen.**

2 HYPHENATION ZONE   [HZone]

The hyphenation zone is the area used to determine if a word is hyphenated or sent to the next line. If more hyphenation is required, increase the zone; if less hyphenation, decrease the zone.

3 JUSTIFICATION   [Just]

The *default* for justification is that it is on, which means that the right side of the page will be exactly lined up. In order to accomplish this, WP adjusts the spaces between words. On the screen the right margin will always look jagged, the line up does not occur until printing takes place. Whether to use justification or not is really up to the user and might also depend upon the document. A justified document is more formal, but in some cases it is also easier to read. Sometimes great white gaps will occur between characters because the justification is being *forced* by the software. If this occurs, it can be corrected by entering soft hyphens thus putting more on a line and reducing white space.

4 LINE HEIGHT   [Line Height]

The line height is the amount of space that each line covers from the very base of one line to the base of the next. It is very dependent upon font, point size, and attribute, that is, bold, italics, etc. This is set on *auto* and unless the user is really eager to spend hours adjusting lines, it should be left on auto. If it is changed, it should be changed to a height measurement that will allow all font types to be used throughout the document without one line printing on top of another.

5 LINE NUMBERING [Ln Num:On]

Line numbering was intended to be used for legal type documents, but librarians will find it useful for counting titles in a bibliography, counting lists of interlibrary loan requests, and for keeping other esoteric library records. When this function is turned on, the line numbers will not appear on the screen, only on the printed page. You will have the option of counting or not the blank lines, of the position of the number, and of restarting the numbering on each page, and of restarting your count every indicated number. This is especially useful for statistical analysis when you want to look at every tenth item in a list.

6 LINE SPACING   [Ln Spacing:#]

The *default* setting for the spaces between the lines is one or single-spaced. This may be changed in fractional or whole number increments. Do not use this command when creating horizontal lines, use Advance instead.

7 MARGINS   [L/R Marg]

If you leave everything as it is originally set up in WP, the margins are one inch all the way around, that is, one inch from the edge of the paper. If you change any margin, all subsequent margins of that type will also be affected by that change. The margins placed before the change will not be affected.

To change the right and left margins, simply enter the margins as numbers. It is not necessary to include the measurement, which is automatic.

8 TAB SET   [Tab Set]

DEFAULT--the default tab set is every .5 inches. This is fine for most applications. These tabs are also left-justified as they would be on a typewriter. But tabs are very easy to change and are a new avenue of creativity for the user.

To change a placement of a tab, clear the entire line by moving the cursor to the far left and deleting to the end of the line--CTRL END. Then simply place an L at every point where you want the tab to occur.

Tabs are normally the left-justified type signified on the tab setting line by L. They can also be right justified (R); they can

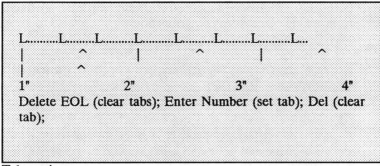

Tab settings

be aligned by the decimal numbers for columns of figures; they can be centered at the tab setting (C); or they can be preceded by dot leader if a Left, Right, or Decimal tab style, by placing a period at the tab.

Whenever you find yourself consistently typing two tabs to get at the right spot on the page, change the tab setting. Part of the usefulness of a word processor is to reduce keystrokes!

REMEMBER--whenever you change a tab setting the rest of the page will be affected after that change. (SEE REVEAL CODES, ALT F3, PAGE 18) A change can be made for a section of a document, and the original tab settings can be re-established by simply calling up the tab setting commands and resetting the original. There is no limit to how many times this can be done, but if it is done too many times, there is probably an easier way to create whatever format.

9 WIDOW/ORPHAN PROTECTION   [W/O]

Widows and orphans are just exactly as you would expect, poor lonely pieces of text left by themselves: widows as single lines of a paragraph at the bottom of a page, and orphans as the only line of a paragraph at the top of the page. This may not be important enough to worry about, although it does have an effect on the smooth readability of a document. The default setting is *no*, meaning that there is no protection against these events occurring. If you feel obliged to prevent this kind of loneliness from taking place, turn the protection on.

2 - Page, see Fig.8-3, Page format.   **1** CENTER PAGE TOP TO BOTTOM   [Center Pg]

This feature is exactly what it seems to be: it centers the text on a page in a vertical perspective. It is important to be sure that the code be entered before all other codes for that page (HOME, HOME, HOME ↑).

Format: Page

    1 - Center Page (top to bottom)   No

    2 - Force Odd/Even Page

    3 - Headers

    4 - Footers

    5 - Margins - Top   1"
                   Bottom   1"

    6 - New Page Number   1
            (example: 3 or iii)

    7 - Page Numbering   No page numbering

    8 - Paper Size   8.5" x 11"
            Type   Standard

    9 - Suppress (this page only)

Fig.8-3, Page format

2 FORCE ODD/EVEN PAGE [Force]

This is a feature that should be used with caution. It is sometimes useful to start a chapter or document with an odd (right) or even (left) page, or if you insist on being really creative, to reverse those concepts. If you force *odd* and the page was already odd, it will start odd. The same goes for *even*. If the page was not odd, it will become the next page number, which, logically, will be odd.

3 HEADERS   [Header]
4 FOOTERS   [Footer]

Headers occur at the top of the page, above the body of text; footers at the bottom, below the text, but not in the margin. Most of the formatting features, including graphics, are possible in the headers and footers. There are options for occurrence: every page, odd pages, even pages. The enigmatic *Header A* and *Header B* simply means that you can create two headers; possibly one for even pages and a different one for odd pages. Please notice that after you select *A* or *B*, it is possible to *edit* a previously created header. Try the examples below; the first section is the text for the header, and the second section is the REVEAL CODES.

SPELL CHECK will also scrutinize the text of headers and footers. Headers and footers will be revealed with VIEW of the print menu. (SEE VIEW DOCUMENT, PAGE 39.)

EXAMPLES
1   April 3, 1990   Library of Tomorrow
- -

^ B[Tab][Date:3 1, 4][Cntr]Library of Tomorrow[C/A/Flrt][Flsh Rt]Technology of today[AdvDn:0.16"][HLine:Left & Right, 6.5", 0.01", 100%]

Library Links   A Continuing Saga   ^ B

[ITALC]Library Links[VLine:2",1.2",7",0.01",100%][Align]A Continuing Saga   ^ B[italc]

5 MARGINS - TOP, BOTTOM [T/B Marg]
The default margins arc 1". To change the top and bottom margin:
> SHFT F8, 2[L], 5[M] number, RETURN, number, RETURN, SPACE BAR or RETURN if completed.

6 NEW PAGE NUMBER   [Pg Num]

At any time within any document, the page numbers can be changed. For instance, if the document starts with an introduction and the page numerals are Roman numerals, the body of the document would typically be paged with Arabic numbers. Wherever this change occurs, use this feature to change the type of numbers and to begin with a certain number. This is also useful if the document is large enough that it can be handled only in two separate files. The second file can pick up the numbering where the first file ended.

REMEMBER: the page number that is on the status line at the bottom of the screen is the number that will be printed on that page; it does not reflect the actual number of pages in the document. If the number type is Roman the status line will give an Arabic status, even though the Roman numeral will be printed on the page.

7 PAGE NUMBERING   [Pg Num Def]

The default is no page numbering. There are nine possibilities for page number placement including a possibility for no number at all. See Fig.8-4, Page number placement.

The placement of page number is as the diagram shows:
> 1 - top left corner
> 2 - top center
> 3 - top right corner
> 4 - even pages--top right corner
>   - odd pages--top left corner
> 5 - bottom left corner
> 6 - bottom center
> 7 - bottom right corner
> 8 - even pages--bottom right corner
>   - odd pages--bottom left corner

To place a page number within a header or footer and therefore control the size and type of the page number, use the header and footer format. (SEE HEADERS AND FOOTERS, PAGE 55.)

CTRL-B (^B) allows the placement of the page number anywhere within the text (including the header or footer). Again this command allows the use of a different type or size of type to distinguish the page number.

8 PAPER SIZE   [PAPER SZ/TYP]
        TYPE

The standard paper size is 8½ x 11, but there are many other possibilities in size. If your printer is not capable of handling different types of paper formats and sizes, obviously it will not be beneficial to change this default. If you do attempt to make the change and an * appears accompanied by a message *Requested Form Unavailable,* go to the Print menu and change the forms. (SEE PRINT, SHFT F7, PAGE 37.)

9 SUPPRESS (THIS PAGE ONLY)   [SUPPRESS]

This command is useful to eliminate headers, footers, and page numbers from a page. All can be suppressed, or several

```
Format: Page Numbering

    Every Page              Alternating Pages

    1   2   3       4               4

                Even            Odd

    5   6   7       8               8

    9 - No Page Numbers
```

Fig.8-4, Page number placement

combinations. This is especially useful for the first page, which traditionally does not have any extraneous information, even though headers, footers, and page numbers are established at the beginning of the document. It is also helpful in a newsletter if there is an ad on a page and it would be more graphically attractive if some or all of this information were eliminated.

3 - DOCUMENT, see Fig.8-5, Document format.

1   DISPLAY PITCH

This feature is dependent upon font and point being used. If this is adjusted incorrectly, text may overlap. This is one of those areas that is best left to WP.

2   INITIAL CODES

This feature allows the defaults for codes to be changed. This is one area that is really safe to ignore.

```
Format: Document

    1 - Display Pitch - Automatic          Yes
                        Width              0.05"

    2 - Initial Codes

    3 - Initial Font          Bits Charter Roman 10pt (ASCII)
                              (Port) (FW)

    4 - Redline Method        Printer Dependent

    5 - Summary
```

Fig.8-5, Document format

3   INITIAL FONT

The font that you have selected to be the default font in the print menu is considered to be the initial font, as opposed to the current font which is whatever font is currently selected. (SEE PRINT, SHFT F7, PAGE 37.)

4   REDLINE METHOD   [RedLn]

Redlining is an editorial concept which means to add or change the marked text. The method of showing this depends upon what the printer is able to do. For instance, if your printer prints in red, redlined areas will appear in red. The HP Laser Series II prints redline as:

Is automation really an effective way to serve...

It may be that this will not be used for editing purposes, but as a graphic feature to highlight text.

5   SUMMARY

The summary is a *sleeper* feature. It very simply allows you to enter basic information about the document: filename, date, subject, author, typist, comments, and a descriptive filename. The date of creation is automatic, and is the first date of work on the document. The comments area is automatically the first 400 characters of the document, but this can be changed to whatever the typist desires. Not only does this help the disk file manager organize the hard disk by providing enough information about a document to determine its value and future existence, it is also a great help when searching for a lost file. When a secretary is entering forty new files every fourteen working days, she may become hard-pressed to create new and imaginative file names. She may start to call files *memo1* or *arp*. Then at 10 am when she has gone to a doctor's appointment, and you are desperate for that file on collection development policy, you will not be able to find it. By using the search feature on **F5** and having implemented the doc summary, it will be a breeze (so speaks the voice of experience). (SEE LIST FILES, F5, PAGE 25.)

4 - OTHER, see Fig.8-6, Other.

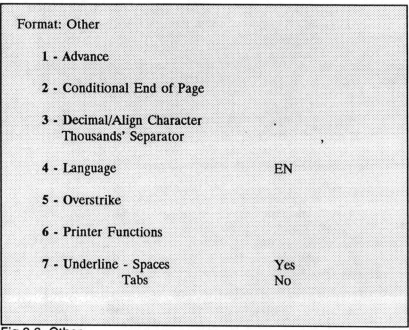

```
Format: Other

    1 - Advance

    2 - Conditional End of Page

    3 - Decimal/Align Character              .
        Thousands' Separator                 ,

    4 - Language                            EN

    5 - Overstrike

    6 - Printer Functions

    7 - Underline - Spaces                  Yes
                    Tabs                     No
```

Fig.8-6, Other

1 ADVANCE   [Adv]

Advance is a new feature for WP. It allows the printer to move a specific distance and direction. It allows the user to move text without depending upon the RETURN key to get you where you want to go. All of the options are available: up, down, right, left. It is also possible to move to a specific point on the page or to a specific line in the current measurement. This is really useful when using horizontal and vertical lines, to prevent the line from going over the top of the text. It also prevents lost text during the reformat process. If you have advanced a line to occur exactly .5" from the previous line, no matter how the text is reformatted, if point size of type is changed, or if graphics are inserted, this line will always appear .5' below the previous line. This control brings the desktop publishing concept to WP.

2 CONDITIONAL END OF PAGE   [Cond EOP]

This command tells WP to either keep a specific number of lines of text together or, if that is not possible, to insert a page break. This is useful to mark the beginning of chapters, to mark passages that are going to be confusing if broken, or to keep a heading connected to the text. This is a much better method than using hard returns or a hard page break to create an artificial page. An artificial page has the potential to haunt the user in later life because, once again, when reformatting occurs, the moving text can cause all kinds of problems, such as the creation of a blank page.

3 DECIMAL ALIGN CHARACTER; THOUSANDS' SEPARATOR   [Decml Char]

This is part of the Math function. As is traditional, a period is used to define a decimal character, and a comma to separate thousands. (As much as I have searched my imagination, I cannot think of any other character for these two placements.)

4 LANGUAGE [Lang]

Obviously the choice of default in the arena of language is the well-renowned English. Although WP claims to be multi-lingual the speller, thesaurus, and hyphenation files are an additional purchase for *foreign* languages. This is the function which lets WP know that a change in language is being made. It is quite possible to switch back and forth between the *alternative* language and English.

5 OVERSTRIKE   [Ovrstk]

Another great feature for foreign language usage, this function allows two characters to be typed in the same space. It is also good for chemical symbols, and for creating one's own unique identifiers. My personal favorite is: ₽. Of course, a more practical use would be: crème de la library.

6 PRINTER FUNCTIONS

Again this is an area where WP probably knows best. If one insists on changing these functions, *kerning* is the amount of space between specific characters. On the old style typewriters, this was not an available feature. Kerning results in a document which has a much more attractive appearance.

7 UNDERLINE[Undrln]

With the availability of italics, the use of underline has become limited. It looks typewriterish. But if it is necessary to use underlines, this command allows the underlining or non-underlining of spaces between words and the space that a tab creates between words. Some typers insist upon using underline to create lines, but that is a WP no-no, use the horizontal line instead.

CTRL F8   controls fonts and their attributes. The options are as follows:

1 Size is controlled by the default font. The choices range from fine to extra large (with five altogether), and a super and subscript. The choices will be determined by the fonts that have been loaded or are available with the program in whatever fashion. You can either experiment and print text in each size or you can look at the printer file to determine exactly what you will create with this choice. You should use these choices rather than a font (4) each time. If you make changes later and change the default, these sizes will go right along with the changes; if you choose the actual fonts, you will have to do major editing. If you are working on a machine that does not have all the fonts available, it will be possible to insert the codes and then use a machine with the various fonts loaded for the actual print job. Again if the attribute codes are inserted, editing will not be a major undertaking. The super and subscript are useful for degree signs and asterisks for highlighting.

2 Appearance gives the option of the font attributes as follows:

1 Bold **bold**

2 Undrln <u>underlines</u>

3 Dbl Und <u>double underlines</u>

4 Italc *italicizes*

5 Outln outlines if your printer is capable

6 Shadw shadows, if your printer is capable

7 Sm Cap PRINTS IN SMALL CAPITALS

8 Redln again, is affected by the printer, but redlines if possible

9 Stkout ~~strikes out text, if possible~~

3 Normal brings the text back to the normal, default font. Remember, it is also possible to leave the attribute selection by moving the cursor to the right and moving over the second code of the pair. This method is much faster and easier.

4 Base Font is the default font, the font upon which all attributes will be based. This should be established at the beginning of the document if the default font is not the preferred font. The default is also set up on the print menu; if you find yourself changing this all the time, it is probably more practical to change the default.

5 Print Color is for those who are fortunate enough to possess a color printer. Because most libraries will not have such an item within their walls, unless it might be a gift from an alum, this will not be discussed at great length. If you do have a color printer, then you can afford to receive full-fledged training and you don't need this book.

ALT F8 known in WP land as Style, is one of the features (the other being graphics) that puts WP in the desktop publishing category. A style is much like a macro in that it is one command that brings forth a combination of codes. The style is primarily formatting codes, whereas a macro will execute, format, or whatever. Styles can be created for every type of document, or one style "set" can be created which will work for all types of documents.

Some style definitions:

style name - the name that WP uses in the style code. Use a name that will make sense to you in the future and that will work as a generic term for all documents. For instance, *title* will signify the main title, *subtitle* will always be a secondary title.

paired - a style which is based on codes which have beginning and ending codes, such as [BOLD][bold]. Because it is necessary to place an end code, this style must be *turned off*.

open - a style which has only a beginning code such as margins, page numbering. This type of style is not *turned off*.

description - whatever details you need to help remember just what this style is for, what it does, or when you should use it - as long as the description does not take more than 54 characters.

enter or return key - in a paired style, the enter key can be a hard return or it can be used to turn a style off or on.

retrieve - all of the styles which you create are stored in one comprehensive style file which must be retrieved into a document. The same file can be retrieved into all documents, but must be loaded once, or you can include this information in the setup feature, **SHFT F1**.

F9

F9   automatically enters the field code ($^\wedge$R) for establishing a secondary file; it also automatically enters the necessary hard return.

SHFT F9   offers the merge code possibilities:
$^\wedge$C; $^\wedge$D; $^\wedge$E; $^\wedge$F; $^\wedge$G; $^\wedge$N; $^\wedge$O; $^\wedge$P; $^\wedge$Q; $^\wedge$S; $^\wedge$T; $^\wedge$U; $^\wedge$V
and gives the opportunity to choose one by an alpha character; it is not necessary to include the $^\wedge$.
The codes stand for:

c	pause for input from keyboard
d	current date
e	end of record
f	field, will also ask for the field number
g	brings up a macro
n	goes to the next record
o	puts a message on the status line
p	inserts a file
q	halts the merge
r	denotes the end of a record
s	goes to the secondary file
t	goes to the printer
u	updates the screen
v	puts merge codes into the document

CTRL F9   initiates a merge or sort. The default sort order is simply *a to z*; *z to a* order would have to be set up.

1 Merge fulfills the need to add different addresses to form letters without having to rekey either the addresses or the letters. Basically it takes a primary file, which is the text file with merge codes marking where the data will go; and the secondary file, which contains the data which will be placed into the marked code areas of the primary file. The secondary file can be used with countless primary files. For instance, a mailing address file can be used to create newsletter labels, to merge with

65

form letters asking for donations, to create lists; a file containing acquisition data can be used to print forms, create acquisition lists, print shelf list cards, and print annotated bibliographies.

2 Sort (see Fig.9-1, Sort menu) rearranges lists or records in alphabetical or numerical order.

--------------------------- Sort by Line ---------------------------

Key Typ Field Word	Key Typ Field Word	Key Typ
Field Word		
1 a 1 1	2	3
4	5	6
7	8	9
Select		
Action	Order	Type
Sort	Ascending	Line sort

Fig.9-1, Sort menu

The sort can be done on a full text file or a blocked area. The sort will be done from the screen, and will place the revised text on the screen unless you indicate otherwise. The default for sorting is by line, which is fine for most applications, but if a bit of information goes to a second line it will be considered a new line. If this situation exists, format the document in a landscape mode which will hopefully put all data on one line, sort, and return to regular portrait mode.

1 Perform action actually executes a sort after the parameters have been established, or the defaults have been accepted.

2 View switches to the actual text file so that you can scroll through the file.

3 Keys are the defined areas which will tell the sort what to do, where, and how. A key is either *a*, alpha, or *n* numeric. The field is the word(s) which is between single tabs. If the sections of a list are not separated by tabs, but by spaces, then the horizontal record will be considered one field. If the three sections are separated by single tabs, then each section will be a field. Within the field, it is possible to further define the sort by word; the words are separated by spaces. Confusion about this distinction often prevents a successful sort. Tabs are much better separators of sections; if the document has been created with spaces, it is worth the time to search spaces, replace with tabs, and then perform the sort.

4 Select allows you to select specific records for sorting which contain specific bits of information. For librarians with online searching experience this will make perfect sense. The options are:

+ or	* and
= exactly same	<> not
> greater than	< less than
>= greater than or equal	<= less than or equal

It is also possible to build strategies with the use of parentheses. As in other search techniques, parenthesized parameters are considered before the un-parenthesized strategy. These strategies are limited to the keys which have already been defined. The statement is typed: key1=[   ] + key4=[   ] with the search word(s) in the brackets. To search all keys for a particular word use keyg=[   ]. This would be useful if you are looking for all addresses in the capital city of the state; if there are none, then you also need to know that. The success of this operation is absolutely dependent upon the correct identification of keys, fields, and words.

5 Action performs the selection if it has been defined. It is possible with this function to select only and not actually sort the records after they have been selected.

6 Order is from A to Z, 0 to 9. A descending order, or reverse of the above, can also be selected.

7 Type defines whether the sort will take place on each line or paragraph of information.

ALT F9   is the graphics feature. The perspective for graphics is the box, of which there are three types: a figure box which contains a graphics picture; a text box which contains textual characters; and a table box which contains maps, graphs, table of numbers, or other data. In addition, there is a user-defined type of box which is anything else outside of the first three; and finally, there is an option for creating horizontal and vertical lines. The box options are:

1 Figure; **2** Table; **3** Text Box; **4** User-defined Box

Within each of these options are the following additional options: create, edit, new number, and options.

1 Create - creates a completely new box. See Fig.9-2, Box menu.

1 Filename - it is possible either to type in the filename or strike **F5**, **F5** to call up the directory and from there retrieve the file. An empty box can be created by omitting a filename.

2 Caption - is created exactly like a footnote or endnote.

3 Type - determines where the box will appear.

> **1** Paragraph will keep the box with the paragraph in which it was created. Place the box code at the beginning of the paragraph, or after the last hard return or hard page. If the box does not fit on the page, it will move to the next page, and the text will fill in the empty space.

2 Page will place the box in an exact position on the page, and it will stay there. Create the box wherever you want it to be positioned, and then enter text to flow around it. Although this may seem easier for layout purposes because the box does not move as it does in the paragraph type, the page type may cause problems during the editing process. If the text associated with the box is moved because of reformatting, font change, whatever, the box will still remain on the page where it was originally positioned. On the other hand, this is appropriate to use if the box contains chapter headers, or information that is not closely related to the text, but is more importantly positioned for its own sake.

3 Character does not actually position a box, but considers that a box is a character. This is great for *big first paragraph character* boxes. These boxes can be created within footnotes and endnotes.

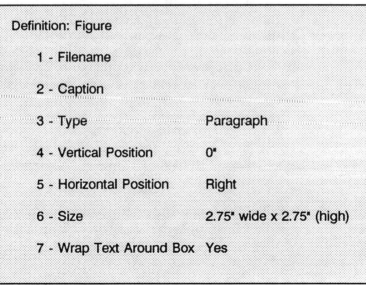

```
Definition: Figure

    1 - Filename

    2 - Caption

    3 - Type                    Paragraph

    4 - Vertical Position       0"

    5 - Horizontal Position     Right

    6 - Size                    2.75" wide x 2.75" (high)

    7 - Wrap Text Around Box    Yes
```

Fig.9-2, Box menu

4 Vertical position depends upon the type. If you want to be even with the paragraph use 0". Remember this type means that you are positioning the box in relationship to the paragraph. If you have chosen page as the type, the options become:

1 Full page; **2** Top; **3** Center; **4** Bottom; **5** Set position.

The first four are obvious, *set position* allows you to place the box by defining the actual inches for the location. This is one of those functions where you can enter cc and WP will convert to inches.

5 Horizontal Position, again, depends upon the type that has been chosen. A paragraph type can be lined up with the right or left edges, centered, or can cross the entire width of the page. A page type is lined with the right or left margins. Choosing columns allows you to line the box up within a column, or to span columns. The set position defines the exact location as a measurement term.

6 Size is automatically determined by WP based on the size of the text file. If you want to change either the width or the height of the box to fit within your perspective of the layout, WP will automatically recalculate the other dimension. It is also possible to manually change both figures, although by doing so you may cut off some of the text; or in the case of a graphic figure, you may skew the figure.

7 Wrap text around box will cause the text to print around the box and not through it. If you want the text to go on as if there were no box, answer this statement in the negative.

8 Edit allows you to edit a box text file with any of the WP formatting codes, or to minimally edit a graphic. Obviously, this is not a draw or paint program, but there are options:

Move - moves the figure across or up and down.

Scale - expands or contracts, horizontally or vertically

Rotate - actually rotates the picture by degrees, clockwise or counter clockwise

Switch - works only for bit-mapped images, reverses black and white

% Change - controls how much change will take place when the above options are used

2 Edit is for editing an already existent box.

3 New Number is for creating a new caption number for a box if you have chosen to number boxes.

4 Options (see Fig.9-3 Box options) is for setting up the default options. This will be in effect for all boxes following this setup.

As with other options, after the options have been determined all boxes will be affected by them. Most of these features are exactly what they appear to be. The *border style*, for which there are seven possibilities, is an instrument of creativity. It is worth considering using a different border style for different types of boxes. For instance, a *sidebar* might have no borders; a *callout* would have a single line on the top and bottom, and no right and left borders. The inside and outside border spaces are margins and affect how closely the text or graphics or surrounding text get to the box. The level numbering allows you to create levels of figures as if they were part of an outline. The style of the caption can be affected by formatting codes. The caption position, again, is an area where you can establish a certain tradition depending upon the contents of the box. Offset is somewhat hard to visualize, because the box is not shown on the screen; but it means that a box will be as close to the paragraph as possible without going to the next page. The minimum offset tells WP how close the box can be moved to the top of the paragraph before WP will force it to the next page. This requires experimentation before expertise. Gray shading is the shading within the box, the closer to 100%, the darker the shading.

Options: Figure

    1 - Border Style
            Left   Single
            Right   Single
            Top   Single
            Bottom   Single
    2 - Outside Border Space
            Left   0.17"
            Right   0.17"
            Top   0.17"
            Bottom   0.17"
    3 - Inside Border Space
            Left   0"
            Right   0"
            Top   0"
            Bottom   0"
    4 - First Level Numbering Method   Numbers
    5 - Second Level Numbering Method   Off
    6 - Caption Number Style   [BOLD]Figure 1[bold]
    7 - Position of Caption   Below box, Outside
                                        borders
    8 - Minimum Offset from Paragraph   0"
    9 - Gray Shading (% of black)   0%

Fig.9-3, Box options

5 Line creates horizontal and vertical lines. The options for both are similar. See Fig.9-4, Line options.

1 Horizontal position aligns the line with right and left margin, either from one to the other, centered, or at a defined position in between. In the case of a vertical line, the horizontal position is still the position between the right and left margins, placing the line to the left or to the right of the left or right margin, between columns, or at a specific distance from the left margin.

2 Vertical position is not applicable to the horizontal line. In the case of the vertical line, it places the line in

Graphics: Horizontal Line

    1 - Horizontal Position   Left & Right

    2 - Length of Line

    3 - Width of Line   0.01"

    4 - Gray Shading (% of black) 100%

Graphics: Vertical Line

    1 - Horizontal Position   Left Margin

    2 - Vertical Position   Full Page

    3 - Length of Line

    4 - Width of Line   0.01"

    5 - Gray Shading (% of black) 100%

Fig.9-4, Line options

relation to the top or bottom margin, centered between these margins, or at a specific distance from the top margin.

2 Length of line; **3** Length of line is exactly that: how long the line will be. This is calculated automatically, but can be controlled manually.

3 Width of line; **4** Width of line determines the thickness of the line. In most cases, this will be a fraction of an inch, or else the line will be overwhelming; again, experimentation is called for.

4 Gray shading; **5** Gray shading is the same function as the shading within a box, except that it is the amount of shading for the line itself. This will be more effective and noticeable as the thickness of the line increases.

F10

F10 SAVE, saves a document without offering the chance to exit and without clearing the screen. This is much more efficient for quick saves, especially if you are one who has a fear of losing the file even though you have timed backup. As with any save function, you have the option of saving on top of the old file and thus replacing the old file, or using a new filename.

SHFT F10 retrieves a document if you know the file name. If you do not, then **F5, F5** will retrieve the whole directory. **SHFT F10** is the more efficient retrieval process for files with known names.

CTRL F10 is the macro function, another one of WP's superb features. A macro is like a batch file; all the commands to execute a certain process are stored in a file that can be called up with a minimum of keying. Macros should be established for any redundant procedure, including salutations, addresses, templates, memos, anything that you find yourself repeating. Macros are also useful to establish consistency among staff members, and to set up some complicated procedures that staff might need to do, but may not know exactly how to do. The process is very simple:

CTRL F10 - define the macro - strike the exact keys that you will be using to call up the macro, for example, the Alt key and a mnemonic key, (ALT I for italics).

- description - this is for the sake of remembering; it is not necessary but it helps to let you know what this macro will do if you forget, or if you leave your position of employment and your replacement needs to know what it does. This is something that we tend to skip, thinking that we will always remember, well, of course, we don't.

- macro def - includes the actual steps of the macro. You just do everything that you would normally do to execute the procedure. When you are finished, press **CTRL F10** to save the macro. To test it, just press the defined macro keys. Remember that a macro will record every keystroke, including back spaces if you make a typo. It is more efficient to either edit or redo the macro; otherwise, every time the macro is executed it will type the typo and then correct it.

To repeat a macro, use the escape key, type the number of repeats desired, and execute the macro. This is great for creating horizontal lines down an entire page. It is also possible to string several macros together, or include one macro as part of the procedure of another.

Most macros are defined as described above, but it is also possible to use macros as if the function were actually a programming language. This feature is for the brave and intrepid.

PART 2:
CREATING DOCUMENTS

In this section, all directions are given to facilitate the creation of certain documents. Each step is detailed with the use of alpha mnemonics as well as numeric keys. Whenever the use of the RETURN or ENTER key is required, the word ENTER is used as that is most consistently seen on keyboards. While it is not necessary to fully understand the features of the various function keys and their combinations to use these examples, the reader is urged to refer to Part 1 of this volume for a complete discussion of keys utilized.

This section is designed primarily for the librarian who prefers to just create the document without knowing why each step was taken and for the librarian who wants to create, yet wants to understand at the same time. Each section could easily be modified to meet any unique needs by following the steps and the explanations together, and making minor modifications to reach a different goal.

Whenever two keys are shown typed together without separation by a comma, they are to be entered together. For instance, *ALT F7* means that the *ALT* key is held down while the *F7* key is typed. Keys typed within brackets are the alpha options. As explained in Part 1, WordPerfect offers the user two ways of selecting the feature, either with a number on the menu or with the alphabetical character associated with the feature. The librarian word-processor should establish a routine to use either alpha or numeric command options for consistency and memory's sake, but of course either works. When data in these examples should actually be typed in, it is printed in italics for clarity.

The samples were designed to be followed step-by-step to create basic, generic documents. Modifications can easily be made by changing page sizes, fonts and font sizes, graphics, and box options. The choices for variety are many without being excessively complicated.

CREATING A LETTER

What you do   What you will get

Step **The letterhead**
1

1.   **F6, SHFT F6**   Bolds, centers text

2.   **CTRL F8, 1 [S], 5 [L]**   Using the default font, changes
                                  the size to large

3.   **ALT F3**   Turns on the Reveal Codes so
                                that the text will be typed within
                                the codes.

4.   Type the address, ending   This will create the address for
      each line with the enter   the letterhead with each line
      key. At the beginning of   bolded, large, and centered.
      each line type **SHFT F6**.
      Stay within the pairs of
      the codes.

Paired codes begin with uppercase words and end with lowercase words.
If you type within these two groups, the code will affect the text. If you
type outside of the codes, the codes will be completely ineffectual.

[BOLD][Cntr][LARGE]School Library System[C/A/Flrt][HRt]
[Cntr]SCT BOCES[C/A/Flrt][HRt]
[Cntr]431 Philo Rd.[C/A/Flrt][HRt]
[Cntr]Elmira, New York 14903[large][bold]
[HLine:Left & Right,6.5",0.01",100%][AdvDn:0.4"][HRt]

Reveal codes for letterhead

5.	**ENTER, ALT F9, 5 [L], 1 [H], F7**	Places a horizontal line across the width of the page, underneath the address.
6.	**SHFT F8, 4 [O], 1 [A], 2 [D], .4, ENTER, F7**	Moves codes, hard returns, text, whatever, down .4" from the horizontal line.
7.	**SHFT F5, 2 [C]**	Inserts a code for the date so that the current date is always reflected on the document.
8.	**F10, *LHEAD***	Saves this file as a template for letterhead. You can use whatever file name will be easiest for you to remember. Anytime that you want to type a letter, just Retrieve (SHFT F10) this file and the letterhead will be there for you to start the text.

Step 2   **Adding a graphic**

9.	**HOME, HOME, HOME UP ARROW, ALT F9, 1 [F], 1 [C], 1 [F], F5, ENTER**, move the cursor to the appropriate. file with a .WPG extension or actually type in the filename, ***BOOK.WPG*, ENTER, 3 [T], 2 [a], 5 [H], 1 [M], 1 [L], 6 [S], 1 [W], 1, ENTER, F7**	Places the cursor at the very beginning of the text, before all codes. Creates a graphic box for a masthead logo, places the BOOK graphic picture in the upper left corner of the page. Reduces the size of the graphic, allows the height to adjust automatically so that if the width is 1", then the graphic will not be askew.
10.	**SHFT F7, 6 [V], F7**	Gives an idea of the view of the page, or what the page will look like when it is printed. The graphic looks odd in the upper left corner, let's move it to the bottom right corner.

11.   **ALT F9, 1 [F], 2 [E], 1, ENTER, 4 [V], 4 [B], 5 [H], 1 [M], 2 [R], F7**   Edits the graphic, changes the vertical position to bottom, changes the margin placement to the right. Now repeat step 10 to see if you like it. Repeat Step 8 to save.

12.   At this point, type in text as you wish. Save the new file under a different name, so that the letterhead will remain intact and uncontaminated.   This may be an appropriate time to practice clearing the screen (F7), and retrieving the letterhead file.

Step 3   **Creating a macro**

13.   **CTRL F10, ALT S, ENTER, Type *Sincerely,* ENTER, ENTER, ENTER, ENTER, *Cynthia LaPier, Director,* ENTER, *ALA1314,* CTRL F10**   Creates a macro for the salutation. At the definition command, actually enter the keys that you will be using to execute the macro. The description is the phrase that will help you to remember that it is this that the macro does. You may skip this step by just striking the Enter key. Please use your own name and title including the necessary punctuation. The ENTER'S in this macro are my own idea of how many lines should be placed between the closing and the name. The electronic mail box number is also a personal choice. The final CTRL F10 saves the macro. Now try it by using the ALT S keys simultaneously.

Step 4   **Printing the letter**

14.   **SHFT F7, 2 [P]**   If the printer has been set up properly, this should be all that is required to print a page.

The result will look like this, although this is a somewhat foreshortened version in an effort to conserve paper:

School Library System
SCT BOCES
431 Philo Rd.
Elmira, New York 14903

February 12, 1989

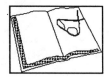

(text)

Sincerely,

Cynthia LaPier, Director
ALA1314

CREATING AN OUTLINE

	What you do	What you will get
Step 1	**Defining the outline**	
1.	**SHFT F5, 6[D]**	The default outline is the typical I, A, 1 form that we all learned how to do in elementary school. If you are satisfied with this format, then it is not necessary to redefine the outline.
2.	**F7, F7**	Inserts the outline definition code in the document, and returns you to the document.
3.	**SHFT F5, 4 [O]**	Turns the outline on, so that an outline level is automatically displayed at every hard return or hard page.
4.	**SHFT F5, 4 [O]**	Retreats from the outline mode. The same command will put you back into outline, wherever it is next entered within the document.
5.	**SHFT F5, 6 [D], 5 [B], F7, 4 [O]**	Creates another outline style, but this time with bullets rather than numbers. Great for lists. See the examples.
6.	**CTRL F2, 2 [P]**	Spell checks the page that you have just entered.

```
I. Library Automation
    A.Needs Assessment
    B.Goals And objectives
        1 . P r o v i d e
        improved patron
        access
        2 . P r o v i d e
        k e y w o r d
        searching
II. Collection Development
    A. Needs Assessment
```
Example outline, traditional

```
•weed collection
        odiscard torn books
        ogive  duplicates  to
        orphanage
        othrow   rest   in
        dumpster
                -tell janitor
                not to bring
                them back
•inventory collection
•convert    collection    to
```
Example outline, bullet

7.   After typing the entire outline, move the cursor back up to II, C (or any higher level). At the end of the text line, strike the **ENTER** key, then **TAB**.

Any time that you want to go back in the outline, the numbers will automatically readjust.

NOTE: Paragraph numbering: SHFT F5, 5[P], Enter or level
is different from the standard outline in that paragraph numbering numbers one number at a time. Although the paragraph numbering can be established to be automatic, usually if every line is numbered, that is considered to be an outline.

When deleting a line, be sure to delete the [Par Num:] code so that the numbers will automatically readjust.

SORTING

	What you do	What you will get
Step 1	**Creating a list**	
1.	*training* *student data* *repeatable fields* *Public Access terminals,* *#* *access time* *software cost* *number of titles/patrons* *MARC input* *MARC output* *field limitation* *integrated* *dial access* *Interlibrary loan* *Cataloguing philosophy* *Boolean searching* *hardware standards* *booking* *multiple collections* *Local Area Network* *Availability status* *keyword searching* *unclear costs* *maintenance costs* *portable barcode* *standard report features* *standard circ.transactions* *user defined reports, etc.* *appendix, other features*	*This will give you a list to work on. Please note that there are no tabs, only spaces between words.*

2.	Place the cursor on the first character of the list, **ALT F4**, move the cursor to the last character, **CTRL F9, 3 [K], (1) a, ENTER, 1, ENTER, 1, ENTER, (2) a, ENTER, 1, ENTER, 2, ENTER, (3) a, ENTER, 1, ENTER, 3, ENTER, F7, 1 [P]**

Blocks the column. This is not necessary as there is no other text in this particular exercise. But if there were a heading, it would be necessary to block all text except the heading, so that the heading would not be sorted also. Defines the keys. The words are all within one field because there are no tab separations. The parameters have been established so that the first three words of each phrase are considered in the sort. Exits the sort definition and actually performs the sort.

3.
access time
appendix, other features
Availability status
booking
Boolean searching
Cataloguing philosophy
dial access
field limitation
hardware standards
integrated
Interlibrary loan
keyword searching
Local Area Network
maintenance costs
MARC input
MARC output
multiple collections
number of titles/patrons
portable barcode
Public Access terminals,
#
repeatable fields
software cost
standard circ. transactions
standard report features
student data
unclear costs
user defined reports, etc.

The list should now look like this.

4.   Enter the following numbers followed by a tab:
2[TAB]access time
5[TAB]appendix, other features
3[TAB]Availabilitystatus
4[TAB]booking
1[TAB]Boolean searching
1[TAB]Cataloguing philosophy
2[TAB]dial access
2[TAB]field limitation
2[TAB]hardwarestandards
2[TAB]integrated
3[TAB]Interlibrary loan
1[TAB]keyword searching
3[TAB]Local Area Network
5[TAB]maintenance costs
1[TAB]MARC input
1[TAB]MARC output
4[TAB]multiple collections
4[TAB]number of titles/patrons
3[TAB]portable barcode
3[TAB]Public Access terminals, #
2[TAB]repeatable fields
4[TAB]software cost
4[TAB]standard circ. transactions
4[TAB]standard report features
3[TAB]student data
2[TAB]unclear costs
3[TAB]user defined reports, etc.

This will give you two fields to work with. It is now a weighted list: 1-5, 1 being a top priority, of automation criteria.

5. Place the cursor on the first character of the list, **ALT F4**, move the cursor to the last character, **CTRL F9, 3 [K], (1) a, ENTER, 1, ENTER, 1, (2) a, ENTER, 2, ENTER, 1, (3) a, ENTER, 2, ENTER, 2, ENTER, (4) a, ENTER, 2, ENTER, 3, ENTER, F7, 1 [P]**

This sets up a sort for the two fields which have been separated by the tab. The first column will be sorted first and then within duplicate areas the second column will be sorted by the first three words.

6.
1	Boolean searching
1	Cataloguing philosophy
1	keyword searching
1	MARC input
1	MARC output
2	access time
2	dial access
2	field limitation
2	hardware standards
2	integrated
2	repeatable fields
2	unclear costs
3	Availability status
3	Interlibrary loan
3	Local Area Network
3	portable barcode
3	Public Access terminals, #
3	student data
3	user defined reports, etc.
4	booking
4	multiple collections
4	number of titles/ patrons
4	software cost
4	standard circ. transactions
4	standard report

The result should be this. These sorts have been done using the block feature; if block had not been used, then the user would have had to choose sort, an input and output *place* (the screen), and then followed the same steps defining the sort.

features
5   appendix,   other
features
5   maintenance costs

RETRIEVING A FILE

What you do	What you will get
Step 1	**The process, using F5**	
1.	F5, F5, scroll through the directory using the arrow keys, highlight a file, **6 [L], F7, 1[R]**	Selects a file, looks at it in a view, non-editing mode, and then loads the text.
Step 2	**An alternative procedure**	
2.	From a blank screen, **F5, F5, N [N]**, enter as many characters of the file name that you know, **ENTER**, move the arrow to the correctly highlighted file, **1 [R]**	Selects a file more efficiently by placing the cursor alphabetically close to the file. This is especially useful if the directory is large.
Step 3	**Another alternative**	
3.	Again, with a blank screen, **F5, F5, 9 [W], 3 [E]**, type in a word pattern that you know is within the file somewhere, **ENTER**.	Retrieves all of the files with the word pattern you have entered, marks them with an asterisk. The file can be viewed before actually being retrieved. This is especially useful when you have completely forgotten the file name, and it didn't make much sense to begin with.

MORE: Try this same exercise with:
    1 [D] to search in just the Document summary
    2 [F] to search the first page

4 [C] to search with a limited set of defined parameters which you establish on the Word Search menu. If you have a large directory, this is faster if you can limit the search to a unique phrase and/or to a range of dates. If you use the Document summary and give every document a subject heading, very librarian-like, author, typist, etc., this feature makes file searching more efficient. This may seem like a waste of time and energy, but the first time you *misplace* a file because you cannot remember the file name or because the file is on your secretary's computer and she is in the Bahamas, this will suddenly seem like the greatest of WP's fine features.

Step 4 **One last alternative**

4. In the presence of a blank screen, **SHFT F10**, type the filename, **ENTER**.

This is for those incredibly organized and efficient colleagues who remember the file name. Obviously this is the ideal retrieval method because it is fast and involves very few steps.

Step 5 **An alternative for non-WP files**

5. **CTRL F5, 1 [T], 3 [e],** filename, **ENTER**

Allows you to retrieve a document that is ASCII DOS formatted. The choice of *3* changes all the carriage returns or line feeds to soft returns.

6. **SHFT F8, 1 [L], 7 [M], 0, ENTER, 0, F7, CTRL F5, 1 [T], 2 [R]**, filename, **ENTER**

Retrieves a text document, but into a file with wider margins so that the format is somewhat closer to what it should be.

NOTES: If the margins of the DOS file are known, the margins of the blank screen should be set as close as possible before retrieval. DOS text or ASCII is usually the format when a file is downloaded from a bulletin board or an online search service. If the text is not formatted correctly, you might use Search and Replace to make formatting revisions.

CREATING A TIMED BACKUP FILE

	What you do	What you will get
Step 1	**Establishing the default**	
1.	**SHFT F1, 1 [B], 1, Y, 10, ENTER, 2 [O], Y, ENTER**	Goes to the setup menu, creates an automatic file backup every ten minutes, also creates a copy of the original file every time the revised file is saved.
2.	**8 [U], 1 [D], ", ENTER, 2 [S], ", ENTER, F7**	Sets the display and perspective in the inch mode. It is quite possible to be creative and use inches for display and points for status line, but it is also more confusing. If you have access to a variety of point sizes, this is best left at inches.

SETTING UP A LANDSCAPE OR HORIZONTAL PERSPECTIVE

What you do

What you will get

Step **The page form definition**
1

1. **SHFT F7, S [S], 3 [E], 4 [F], cursor to** *All Others*, **3 [E], 1 [W], 11, ENTER, F7, F7, F7, F7, F7**

Takes you to the edit mode for the printer definition and establishes the widest form as 11", which is the typical size of paper. If you want to use a longer sheet and your printer will not whine and complain, enter a larger number here.

2. **SHFT F8, 2 [P], 8 [S], 2, [t], 1 [S], F7**

Changes the format of the page to landscape. At this point REVEAL CODES should show you this code: [Paper Sz/Typ:11" x 8.5",Standard] which means that the width is 11", the height is 8.5", and the paper bin or feeder is the one containing standard type paper. The last menu of paper type choices are not applicable to those of us with only one paper feeder.

REMEMBER: If you want to change back to regular paper, just delete the [Paper Sz/Typ...] code. It's possible to add this to a document at any time and at any place. During font creation choose both portrait and landscape fonts or none of this will work. It should be necessary to set up the landscape mode as an option only once. If a message appears:
* Requested Form Unavailable, then you have offended the paper gods; you must return to the printer definition edit menu and reestablish the set-up for paper of a width greater than 8.5".

CREATING COLUMNS

	What you do	What you will get
Step 1	**The newspaper column definition**	
1.	**ALT F7, 4 [D]**	Brings up the column definition menu.
2.	**1 [T], 1 [N],** {Newspaper}, **2 [N] 3, ENTER, 3 [D], .5, ENTER**	Newspaper columns go down one column, wrap around to the next, go down the second column, and so on. For experiment's sake, set up a page with three columns, and .5" between each column.
3.	**4 [M], ENTER, F7, 3 [C]**	The margins are automatically adjusted for three equal columns. It is only necessary to change this if you want columns to be of unequal width, or if you want to change the margins for some strange reason. (Actually it would be easier to change the margin with SHFT F8, etc., first, and then set up the columns - let WP do the calculations for you.) Exits the column definition menu, and turns columns on.
4.	Either type in lots of text or Retrieve a previously created file with **SHFT F10** filename, or with **F5, F5**, highlight filename, **1 [R]**.	As long as text is entered, after the columns are defined, it will be affected by the column codes until the codes are turned off.

5.   Somewhere, anywhere,   Turn the columns off.
within the text, **ALT F7,
3 [C].**

This is what this activity might have looked like:

A PRIMER FOR THE SCHOOL L I B R A R Y M E D I A SPECIALIST WHAT DOES ALL THIS OPTICAL DISC TALK MEAN C D - R O M , compact disc read-only-memory, is a 4.7 inch read-only optical memory disc. It stores up to 600 megabytes of computer data and audio (yellow book), is very similar to the music compact-disks. There is an additional level of error correction on the cd-rom, a higher degree of data integrity, data is on the disc instead of audio information, and the software updates are stored on a floppy disk. In order to differentiate

between an optical and a floppy format computer people are using 'disc' for optical and 'disk' for floppy applications.

**Step
2**   **The parallel column
definition**

1.   **ALT F7, 4 [D], 1 [T], 2
[P], 2 [N], 2, ENTER, 3
[D], .5, ENTER, 4 [M],
F7, F7, 3 [C]**   This sets up a parallel type
column format for two columns
with .5" between the two columns.
The margins are based on the
established margins for the
document.

2.   Enter *Goals*, **CTRL
ENTER**, *Objectives*, **CTRL
ENTER**   You have entered the headers for
the columns. The CTRL
ENTER's have created [HPg]
codes in the document which will
result in columns if the column
feature is turned on.

3.   Enter text. After each
section, use **CTRL-
ENTER.**   These pages were created with
parallel text format.

SEARCHING AND REPLACING

	What you do	What you will get

Step 1   **The process, using text**

1.	**F5, F5,** highlight a file, **1[R], ENTER**	Loads a text file, any file will do.
2.	**ALT F2, Y**	Initiates the search and replace process, tells the program not to make a change unless it is confirmed by the user.
3.	**the, F2, witch, F2**	Tells the program to search for all occurrences of the word *the* and replace them, if confirmed, with the word *witch*.
4.	Either **Y,** or **N,**	Continues the search after the first *hit*, either replacing or not, as you wish.

NOTE: The cursor has to be at the very beginning of the text in order to find all the words being searched. When searching for a word that is a part of another word, or a common syllable in some way, answer the confirm statement in the affirmative. If the search is very esoteric or unusual, you will probably be safe with a negative response to affirm. It is especially important when replacing acronyms with the full-fledged phrase to be sure that the acronym itself is not a common syllable. Search and replace is great, but it does correct capitalization problems.

Step 2   **the process, using codes**

5.	Using the same text file as in the above example,	Puts the cursor in position at the beginning of the text. The third HOME makes sure that the

	HOME, HOME, HOME ↑	cursor also goes to the very beginning of the codes.
6.	**ALT F2, y, CTRL ENTER,** **F2, CTRL ENTER, CTRL** **ENTER**	Establishes the search and replace parameters which are to confirm each replacement, looks for all hard returns and replaces them with two hard returns. Enter the CTRL and ENTER together, [HRT] should appear on the search line. This might be useful to put double spacing between paragraphs of a single-spaced document, as an afterthought.
7.	**HOME, HOME, ↑, ALT** **F2, Y, SPACE, SPACE,** **F2, SPACE**	Reverses the above process, replaces all double spaces with a single space. Maybe you didn't like the way it looked, or you have decided to send the article electronically and blank lines take up precious time and accomplish nothing.

NOTE: Code replacement works with most codes. It is very useful to replace the hard pages created by a merge with hard returns, to replace spaces with tabs, to replace double spaces which create white rivers in documents with single spaces, to replace occurrences of normal text with italicized, bold, or both. For instance, it comes in handy if you are working on an automation document and you decide that you want to go back and emphasize *MARC*. The uses for this feature are really limited only by one's imagination.

BLOCKING, MOVING AND COPYING

	What you do	What you will get
Step 1	**Blocking and moving pieces of text**	
1.	SHFT F10 or F5, F5, 1 [R]	Retrieve a text file on which to work the wonders of blocking. moving, and copying text
2.	Place the cursor on the second sentence, ALT F4, highlight the first four words.	Blocks part of a sentence. Remember - you can block by moving the cursor, by using the return key, by paging down or up, or by typing the character which is the end of the intended block.
3.	CTRL F4, 1 [B], 1 [M]	Moves the block from the spot at which it currently resides.
4.	Move the cursor to any other place on the page, ENTER.	Retrieves the text at the spot where the cursor is now.
Step 2	**Changing textual characteristics through blocking**	
5.	ALT F4, move cursor over several words	Blocks the area to be changed.
6.	CTRL F8, 2 [A], 4 [I]	Italicizes the blocked area.
7.	CTRL F10, ALT I, ENTER, CTRL F8, 2 [A], 4 [I], CTRL F10	Creates a macro to italicize text.

8.	**ALT F4**, move cursor over several words, **ALT I**	Blocks an area and with the macro, italicizes it.

NOTE: It is possible to repeat this process for any font alternative within the size and character options. Blocking text to make bold or to change to uppercase or lowercase, follows the same basic steps.

Step 3	**Moving a sentence, a paragraph, or a page**	
9.	Place the cursor anywhere within a sentence, **CTRL F4**, 1 [S], 1 [M]	Highlights the whole sentence to be moved, copied, or deleted.
10 .	Move the cursor to a different location, **ENTER.**	Retrieves the whole sentence at the new location. Obviously, this technique is much faster than using the block and copy. This works if you want to move the whole sentence rather than just a part of a sentence, paragraph, or page.
11.	**ALT F4**, highlight an area of text, **CTRL F4**, 1 [B], 2 [C]	Highlights a block of text and defines that it will be copied, that is, the original text will remain in place and will be repeated elsewhere.
12.	Move the cursor to a new location, **ENTER**	Retrieves the text.
13.	**CTRL F4**, 4 [R], 1 [B]	Retrieves the text again.
14.	**SHFT F10, ENTER**	A quick and easy way to copy the text again.

It is also possible to use the block feature to move codes. It will be necessary to use ALT F3 to reveal the codes and to be sure that they are being highlighted as desired.

Now for a real practice session. Create a petition for patrons to sign to get your local government officials to give the library more funding. Your assignment: center the heading, write your pitch paragraph, create two columns, one for names and one for addresses, then:

15.   ALT F9, 5 [L], 1 [H], F7, SHFT F8, 4 [O], 1 [A], 2 [D], .6, ENTER, F7, move the cursor to beginning of the horizontal line code, ALT F4, highlight the line and the advance codes, CTRL F4, 1 [B], 2 [C], ENTER, SHFT F10, ENTER, repeat SHFT F10, ENTER to the bottom of the page.

Creates a horizontal line followed by .6" of space, blocks the codes for this, copies the codes, and then repeats the copy until the page is covered with lines.

CREATING A STYLE

What you do   What you will get

Step **The style, paired**
1

1. **ALT F8, 3 [C], 1 [N],**   Brings up the style menu, creates
    header, **ENTER, 2 [T], 1**   a style with a name and a
    [P], 3 [D], *a larger point,* description, designates it a paired
    bold, italics, to use for   style, and takes you into the code
    headings, **ENTER, 4 [C]**   screen.

2. **F6, CTRL F8, 4 [B],**   Sets up codes for bold, a larger
    (select a font that is two   font, and italics, exits the code
    sizes larger than the   screen, saves the style as a file.
    default font), **1 [S], CTRL**   **TIP:** Use a file extension when
    F8, 1 [S], 5 [L], CTRL   saving to avoid confusion later on
    F8, 2 [A], 4 [I], move the   in life. For instance, an extension
    cursor past the   of *.sty* will immediately remind
    [Comment], **F7, 6 [S]**,   you that this is a style file. It will
    enter a filename, **F7**.   also allow you to use the same
                                       filename for other types of files,
                                       that is, the text might be book,
                                       the macros, book.mac, the style,
                                       book.sty, the master document,
                                       book.mas., primary merge files,
                                       book.pf, secondary merge file,
                                       book.sf. In all possible cases,
                                       make your word processing life
                                       easier by organizing!

It is possible to create more formats within this one style file. Style is a
good method for changing font types. When fonts are changed in a
macro, because of the method of selection, execution is not always
possible. Some basic rules about headers or headings are that they should
be no more than two points larger than the body text, and that they
should be the opposite type of serif from the body text. In other words,

if the text is 10 point Dutch Roman, then the header should be 12 point Swiss.

REMINDER: If you want to make a global change of styles, it is very easy to edit the code definition and, in effect, change all the headers or whatever at once. This is really useful when changing machines, from one with a small variety of fonts to one with more variety.

Step 2   **the style, open**

3.   ALT F8, 3 [C], 2 [T], 2 [O], 1 [N], format, ENTER, 3 [D], enter description if desired, 4 [C], SHFT F8, 1 [l], 7 [m], 1.5, ENTER, 1.5, ENTER, 8 [t], CTRL END, L, move cursor to inch locations and enter L, F7, 2 [P], 5 [M], 1.00, ENTER, 1.00, ENTER, F7, ALT F7, 4 [D], 1 [T], 1 [N], N, 2 [N], 2, ENTER, 3 [D], 0.5, ENTER, 4 [M], F7, F7, 3[C], F7, F7, 6 [S], BOOKS.STY, ENTER, if asked to replace previous file, respond [Y]es

Creates an open style which establishes a right and left margin of 1.5", a tab set of 1", top and bottom margins of 1", and sets up a two column newspaper type format.

CREATING A MASTHEAD

What you do   What you will get

Step   **Creating the style**
1

1. **ALT F8, 3 [C], 1 [N],**   Labels style as being a paired
    MASTHEAD, ENTER,   style which will be used for the
    2 [T], 1 [P], 3 [D]   masthead.
    MASTHEAD FOR
    NEWSLETTER, ENTER,
    4 [C]

2. **CTRL F8, 4 [B], N [N],**   Changes the font to a large size
    enter the name of a sans   for effect.
    serif font of 24 or 36
    point, **ENTER, 1 [S], F7,**
    or use **CTRL F8, 1 [S], 7**
    [E]

3. **SHFT F8, 4 [O], 6 [P],**   Creates spacing between the
    3 [W], 3 [P], 150,   words and letters of the masthead.
    ENTER, 3 [P], 250,   If you feel there is too much
    ENTER, F7, move the   white space between either the
    cursor to the right of the   words or the letters, just reduce
    [COMMENT].   the percentage for either or both.

4. **SHFT F8, 4 [O], 1 [A],**   Moves the text down to the 1.5
    3 [i], 1.5, ENTER, F7,   inch line on the page, not down
    ALT F9, 5 [L], 1 [H], 1   1.5 inches, but to the 1.5 spot
    [H], 4 [B], 3 [W], .25,   from the top edge of the paper.
    ENTER, 4 [G], 40,   Creates a horizontal line that is
    ENTER, F7, SHFT F8, 4   .25" in width, and is not all black,
    [O], 1 [A], 2 [D], .3,   but only 40% black. The text will
    ENTER, F7, F7, 6 [S]   be forced down another .3" after
                                  the horizontal line.

NOTE: These measurements are arbitrary. You will want to make
creative graphics decisions determined by a good sense of taste and style.

CREATING A BOX WITH A DROP SHADOW EFFECT

	What you do	What you will get
Step 1	**The box option definition**	
1.	ALT F9, 1 [F], 4 [O], 1 [B], S, T, S, T	Sets up the option to create a box with a left and top single line and a right and bottom thick line.
2.	3 [I], .5 ENTER, .5 ENTER, .5 ENTER, .5 ENTER, ENTER	Creates an inside margin of .5"
3.	ALT F9, 1 [F], 1 [C], 3 [T], 2 [a], 4 [V], 3 [C], 5 [H], 1 [M], 3 [C], 6 [S], 3 [B], 4, ENTER, 5, ENTER	Creates a box that is 4" by 5" and is centered on the page horizontally and vertically.
4.	Either 8 [E] and enter text or 1 [F] and enter the filename, F7	Places text within the box.
5.	SHFT F7, 6 [V]	Lets you look at your masterpiece.

NOTE: If you want the thick sides to be even thicker use 7 [E] instead of 5 [H].

Step 2	**Creating a spectacular text file for this box**	
6.	SHFT F8, 4 [O], 6 [P], 3 [W], 3 [P], 200, ENTER, 3 [P], 200, ENTER until exited	Sets the default for the spacing so that it is increased between letters and words.

7. **CTRL F8, 4 [B]**, move cursor to a font size of 14 pt or greater

    Establishes a font for the text.

8. Enter text as desired. If not inspired to greatness, try: *INVITATION* **ENTER,** *Come to the Open House at Great Memorial Library* **ENTER,** *See the unveiling of the electronic card catalog. May 14, 1989, 6:00 pm*

    Creates an invitation to an open house.

9. Save the file, edit the box as shown in figure 1 and retrieve with **1 [F]**. Create figure 2, the clapping hands, using the following codes for the graphic within the box.

The Codes: The following codes are what would appear at **ALT F9, 1** [F]igure, **2** [E]dit for each figure on the previous page. (Text) appears instead of a filename because the text was entered directly from **8** [E]dit on this same menu.

INVITATION

Come to the
Open House at
Great Memorial
Library

See the
unveiling of the
electronic card
catalog.

May 14,
1989, 6:00 pm

Figure 1 (text), Figure 2 (graphic)

The following are the definitions for the figures. They should appear on the screen with **ALT F9, 1** Figure, **2 Edit**. This is the information which defines the placement on the page and the size of the figure. At this screen these details can be revised to change placement or size.

Definition: Figure 1

1 - Filename	(Text)
2 - Caption	
3 - Type	Page
4 - Vertical Position	Center
5 - Horizontal Position	Margin, Center
6 - Size	4.05" wide x 5" high
7 - Wrap Text Around Box	Yes
8 - Edit	

Definition: Figure 2

1 - Filename	APPLAUSE.WPG (Graphic)
2 - Caption	
3 - Type	Page
4 - Vertical Position	6.5"
5 - Horizontal Position	Margin, Center
6 - Size	1.5" wide x 1.5" high
7 - Wrap Text Around Box	Yes
8 - Edit	

CREATING INTERCOLUMNAR VERTICAL LINES

	What you do	What you will get
Step 1	**Defining the columns**	
1.	**ALT F7, 4 [D], F7, 3 [C]**	Defines the columns by accepting the defaults.
2.	**HOME, HOME, HOME,** ↑	Moves the cursor to the beginning of the document, that is, not only before the text but also before all of the codes.
3.	**ALT F3**, move cursor to the immediate position after the column definition	Places the cursor in the appropriate place for all of this to work.
4.	**ALT F9, 5 [L], 2 [V], 1 [H]3 [B], ENTER, 2 [V], 5 [S], 2, F7, F7**	Places a vertical line immediately after the first column, and two inches down. You could also use Set position, which would place the line at the top of the page of text.

NOTE: If you have more than one column, repeat step 4, and instead of ENTER, key in the number of the column the line is to follow and then ENTER. Repeat for as many columns as you have established.

Placing the lines within a header, avoids repeating the definition for every page. This technique is great for a newsletter in which you want the vertical lines on every page.

If you make the vertical line Header A and the rest of the header Header B, then you can use **SHFT F8, 2 [P], 9 [u]** to suppress the header containing the vertical lines if for some reason you do not want them to appear on a certain page, but you do wish to retain the rest of the header information. This might be appropriate if you were going to use a one-column format for a particular story, or if you were going to include a graphic that covered all of the columns.

CREATING A TABLE OF CONTENTS

What you do   What you will get

Step   **Determining the levels of**
1   **the table**

1.   **ALT F5, 5 [D], 1 [C], 1**   Creates a table of contents with
      [N], 2, 2 [D], N, 3 [P],   two levels, heading and
      5 [L], 3 [(], F7, F7   subheading. The second level will
                                      not wrap around. The page
                                      numbers for the first level will be
                                      flush right with dot leaders, and
                                      the second level will be
                                      immediately followed by the page
                                      number in parentheses.

2.   Within the text, find the   Blocks and marks the appropriate
      text which will be included   text to be the first level for the
      in the Table of Contents,   Table of Contents. The same
      ALT F4, highlight the   procedure is followed for the
      appropriate text, **ALT F5**, second level, a "2" replacing the
      1 [C], ENTER, 1   "1."

NOTE: If you use the style format for headings and subheadings, it is
possible to include the code for the Table of Contents in the style
definition. This code can be added after the fact and will have a global
effect on the document; or, if you are really organized, it can be added
when the style is first created. This is the fastest and most convenient
way to mark text especially when you are already using style identifiers
such as headings and subheadings.

Step   **Creating a style with a**
2   **table of contents code**

3.   **ALT F8, 7 [R]**, enter   Defines the style to the point
      filename, **ENTER, 3 [C]**,   where you will actually put in the
      1 [N], headertoc, **ENTER,** codes.

2 [T], 1 [P], 3 [D], a header which will be marked for TOC, level 1, **ENTER, 4 [C]**

4.   **ALT F4,** move cursor to the right of the [COMMENT], **ALT F5, 1 [C], 1,** move cursor back to beginning of codes, **F6, CTRL F8, 1 [S], 5 [L]**

In order to set the table of contents codes, it is necessary to turn the block on. You must move the cursor after the comment or else the code will not affect the text. Then to enter other codes, bold and large, go back to the beginning and put in the codes.

5.   **F7, F7, 6 [S], F7**

Returns to the text.

Step 3   **Generating the table of contents**

6.   Place the cursor at the beginning of the text, **ALT F5, 6 [G], 5 [G], y**

The table will be generated wherever the cursor is blinking; unless you want it in the body of the text, place the cursor at the beginning. Generation should be done upon completion of the document. If you do do it before completion and have to redo, you will have the option of replacing the original generation. This procedure may take some time if the document is lengthy, so do not start generating five minutes before you are going to go home.

CREATING AN INDEX

What you do

What you will get

Step 1 **Defining the index**

1. **ALT F5, 5 [D], 3 [I], Index, ENTER, 3 [(], F7**

Place the index definition at the end of the document. Use CTRL-ENTER to create a new page, enter a heading or title, and then define. Sets up the index format as one in which the entries are followed immediately by the page numbers enclosed by parentheses. As you have seen on the index menu there are the following additional options:
1 - No Page Numbers
2 - Page Numbers Follow Entries

[3 - (Page Numbers) Follow Entries - our choice]
4 - Flush Right Page Numbers
5 - Flush Right Page Numbers with Leaders

Also creates an index which will be a concordance. A concordance means that the index words do not have to be marked within the document, instead a file is created that is just a list of all the words to be considered in the index. When the generation takes place, the list is compared to the document and the index is created. This is incredibly simple, but it is limited by the amount of RAM available to do the generation. If you have a really complicated index to create, use the concordance for those words or phrases that are repeated often or that would be considered index headings as opposed to index sub-headings. Then move to Step 2.

Step **Creating the index**
2

2. **ALT F5, 3 [I], enter word, Automation, ENTER, Circulation, ENTER**

While inputting text, allows you to mark the spot for an index reference. In other words as you are typing the word *circulation*, you decide that you want an index entry to be created under the heading: Automation, and the subheading: Circulation.

3. Move cursor to a keyword, **ALT F4,** move cursor to highlight word(s), **Alt F5, 3 [I], ENTER, ENTER**

Marks the text after the fact, after the document has been typed. First it is necessary to block the text. WP then assumes that the word that has been blocked is the index heading. If it is not, simply retype the correct heading. The same applies to the subheading; if none is desired, strike the Enter key to complete the process.

Step **Generating the index**
3

4. Place the cursor at the end of the text, **ALT F5, 6 [G], 5 [G], y**

The Index will be generated wherever the cursor is blinking. Generation should be done upon completion of the document. This may take some time if the document is lengthy, so do not

start five minutes before you are
going to go home. (Sound
familiar?)

NOTE: If you will recall, when you defined the index you gave the
concordance a file name. When the index is generated, the concordance
information is what directs WP to go back to that file as well as to
recognize all index marks within the document. If you have forgotten to
include the concordance name, the words within that file will not be
included in the index unless you go back to the beginning of the
document and redefine the index, or unless you mark all the words as
index items.

CREATING A MACRO THAT WILL CALL UP A STYLE

What you do	What you will get

Step 1   **Creating the macro**

1.	**CTRL F10, ALT H,** heading style, **ENTER, ALT F8,** {note: this will only work if a style is already present} **N, HEADING, ENTER, 1 [O], CTRL F10**	Creates a macro that will automatically call up the style for a heading that also marks the text for table of contents. This is one of the easiest features in WP, and one of the greatest time savers. Use macros for the styles that you find you use all of the time. A one time use style, such as the masthead, is not appropriately macroed because of space and limited mnemonics

NOTE: If you use one main style for all documents, then use SHFT F1, 7 [L], 6 [L], filename, F7. The style will be automatically retrieved with all documents, and this macro will always work.

CREATING BOOKMARKS

	What you do	What you will get
Step 1	**Setting the framework**	

1.	ALT F7, 4 [D], 1 [T], 1 [N], 2 [N], 3, ENTER, 3 [D], 1, F7, F7, 3 [C]	Sets up a four column page with one inch between each column, lets WP figure the margins.
2.	ALT F9, 5 [L], 2 [V], 1 [H], 3 [B], 1, F7, F7	Puts a vertical line after the first column. REPEAT this step, substituting 2, 3 for each column number.
3.	ALT F9, 1 [F], 1 [C], 1 [F], BOOK.WPG, ENTER, 3 [T], 2 [a], 4 [V], 4 [B], 5 [H], 3 [S], 1.25, 6 [S], 3 [B], 1, ENTER, 1, ENTER, F7	Creates a figure with the book graphic (the only one that WP includes in its free clip art set that even remotely suggests library). Places the graphic on the bottom of the page and .25" within the first column's right margin. Makes the graphic 1" by 1" so that it will fit.
4.	ALT F3, Move cursor to the code ([Figure:1; BOOK.WPG;]) for the graphic code, ALT F4, move cursor to the right, CTRL F4, 1 [B], 2 [C], ENTER, SHFT F10, ENTER, SHFT F10, ENTER, SHFT F10, ENTER	Copies the graphic box four times for each column. If you used SHFT F7, 6 [V] at this time, you would see only one graphic figure.

116

5.   **ALT F9, 1 [F], 2 [E], 2, ENTER, 5 [H], 3 [S], 3.75, ENTER, ALT F9, 1 [F], 2 [E], 3, ENTER, 5 [H], 3 [S], 6.25, ENTER, ALT F9, 1 [F], 2 [E], 4, ENTER, 5 [H], 3 [S], 8.75, ENTER, F7**   Edits the three boxes so that the horizontal position for each is within .25" of the column's right margin.

6.   **ALT F9, 3 [B], 4 [O], 1 [B], 2 [S], 2 [S], 2 [S], 2 [S], 9 [G], 0, ENTER, F7**   Creates a text box option with four sides of single lines and a white background.

7.   **ALT F9, 3 [B], 1 [C], 3 [T], 2 [a], 5 [H], 3 [S], 6 [S], 3 [B], 1.5, ENTER, 5, ENTER, F7**   Creates the first text box, connected to the page, in line with the left margin of the first column, 1.5 " wide because that is the width of the column, and 5" in height because that is the guess.

8.   Move the cursor to highlight and so to block the text box, **ALT F4, CTRL F4, 1 [B], 2 [C], ENTER, SHFT F10, ENTER, SHFT F10, ENTER, SHFT F10, ENTER**   Blocks and copies the box three more times.

9.   **ALT F9, 3 [B], 2 [E], 2, ENTER, 5 [H], 3 [S], 3.5, ENTER, F7**   Edits box 2, so that it is flush with the left margin of the column. Repeat this editing procedure for the other boxes. Adjust box 3 so that the horizontal set position is 6"; box 4 so that it is 8.5."

NOTE: We have created empty boxes, now it will be necessary to go back into each box, edit, and use 8 [E] to enter text in each box. If you want each bookmark to be exactly the same, enter the text before step 9, so that the text will also be copied.

Welcome to the Empire Library.

Hours: 8am - 5pm
    Mon - Fri

Reference Desk Phone Service
(xxx) xxx-xxxx

The Empire Library provides:
Interlibrary Loan Services
Large Print Books
Young Adult Programs
AV and CD Loans
Overdue Amnesty Days
Exhibits by Local CraftsPeople

The Empire Library

Stroy Hours every day from 10am - 11am

Mothers-
    Be There!

CREATING REFERENCES

	What you do	What you will get
Step 1	**Marking the reference during input**	
1.	Type: *The development of the five year plan for the Empire Library was based upon the mission statement (see Mission Statement, page 34, **SPACE**).*	Gives you sample text to work with. Automatic references can always be added after the fact by placing the cursor at the right spot and using ALT F5. The page number will be inserted by the program during the generating process.
2.	**ALT F5, 1 [R], 1 [R], 1 [P],** *Mission Statement,* **ENTER**	Places a code for an automatic reference to *Mission Statement* and its page number. After the code is imbedded, finish the text with a space for the page number, an end parentheses, and a period.
3.	Move the cursor to the text where Mission Statement would occur, **ALT F5, 1 [R], 2 [T], ENTER**	Places the code for the target at the appropriate place. If you do this immediately after marking the reference, the target word or phrase will appear automatically.

NOTE: This procedure should also be used to make references to targets such as figures and boxes. One reference can have several targets, for instance, the targets might be text and a figure.

4.	Within document, type: *Figure*, **ALT F5, 1 [R], 1 [R], 5 [G], 1 [F], ENTER**	Marks a reference for which the target is a figure box.

NOTE: It is useful to use Search to find the reference and target words or phrases quickly. When the search locates one, enter the code, and use F2, F2 again to continue the search.

Step 2	**Generating the references and targets**	
5.	**ALT F5, 6 [G], 5 [G], y**	The same process as generation of indexes and Table of Contents. Again, it does take some time. It is most effective to plan to do the generation for all at one time, especially since each subsequent generation will eliminate all previous generations.

WORKING WITH FONTS

What you do

Step   **Creating the fonts**
1

1.   It is necessary to use an additional software package, such as Bitstream's Fontware, to create fonts other than those that are resident in the printer. Assuming that you are working with an HP Laser Jet Series II printer, the residential fonts are Courier, and some line printer fonts. Needless to say, creativity is limited by this minimal selection. Bitstream provides an installation program and three typefaces: Dutch, Swiss, and Charter for registered owners of WP 5.0. This is definitely worth the phone call. It is necessary to have a version of WP dated 7/11/88 or later in order for the fonts to work. Another good reason to register your software, so that you can receive updates and upgrades!

Before trying to create fonts, make sure that there are no resident programs, such as, SideKick, loaded. Ram resident programs have a tendency to cause problems. Creating fonts takes the computer a **long** time. Even a machine with a 286 processor and 20 mhz takes about two hours to create 182 fonts. If possible, it is sometimes better to let the machine do its thing at night while you are home enjoying your family.

Put the fontware floppy in drive a, and from a DOS C prompt, type *A:FONTWARE*, and **ENTER**. Answer the monitor question. Highlight and press enter on the SET UP FONTWARE line. The next menu requires you to select directories for the files. It is a good idea to use whatever the documentation suggests, for example:

for the fontware software	C:\fontware
for WordPerfect	C:\WP50
for the actual fonts	C:\fonts

The fontware software files can be deleted after you have finished creating fonts, if you do not plan to add more fonts at another time. You may also decide to delete depending upon how much space you have on your drive.

The fonts should go in a file by themselves. Fontware creates a font and a backup font file; it is very confusing to have both of these files for every created font in the WP directory. They clutter up the directory and cause confusion. Put them in a separate place.

Next choose your printer, and if the printer has the capability of both landscape and portrait, (sideways and up-and-down), choose that option. If you think you won't need both, don't kid yourself--you will.

There are three disks for typefaces. It will be necessary to load each typeface as the next step. Each typeface has four choices: Roman, Italic, Bold, Bold Italic. Use all of them, for it is extremely frustrating not to be able to use bold or italic for the point sizes that you will be using. There is a tendency for users to assume that the bold and italic choices automatically come with the base font: they don't, they must be created.

Adding fonts is the time-consumer. You can create point sizes of any number from 6 and up, and in fractions if desired. The easiest sizes to deal with are the even numbers, because that is what most printers use. A point size of 8 is appropriate for a caption, 10 for magazine and newsletter type documents, 12 for letters or memos to be read by people with average eyesight, 14 for headers, 24 for overheads, and anything larger for posters or signs. The larger the size of the font, the bigger the size of the file. In other words, if your disk doesn't have much space, don't create a lot of large point fonts. Or make a decision that you will create only bold and bold italic for the 36 point size because they are really the only effective choices for posters. For the 10, 12, 14, and possibly 8 sizes, you will find it necessary to create all four choices for each, whether Dutch or Swiss. Bit Charter is a typeface that was created for computer use. It is very close to the Dutch, so you might decide to skip that one.

Any time during the process of entering size, it is possible to press **F6** to determine how much time you will need to create what you have so far specified and if you have enough space.

When you are finished press **F10**, again you will get a time and space message.

Hours later, when the fonts are created, and assuming that there were no glitches, it is now necessary to let WP know that they exist. Go to the printer menu, **SHFT F7, S [S], 3 [E], 7 [D]**, enter *C:\FONTS* if it is not already there, **5 [C]**, highlight Soft Fonts, **ENTER**. This step takes a long time, do not hit ENTER again in impatience; it will cancel and you will have to start over again, (so says the Voice of Experience). For fonts preceded by (FW), mark them with a **+** or and *****. Using the ***** loads the font during the first print job and does not load it again; this is efficient but takes up memory. If you are networking the printer, it will be helpful to come to a consensus on who will mark what file with an *****, and who will initialize the printer. The **+** will load the file every time that it is used in a print job. This takes longer for each print job, but that time may prove to be negligible and less trouble free in the long run. **F7** your way out of all the menus and the selection will be saved.

When you select the Initial Font on the printer menu, in effect, you are telling WP that that is the font to which the program will default for every document. This should be the font that you will be using most of the time. Keep in mind that readers find it easier to scan fonts with a serif (Dutch), and that a sans serif font should be used for headlines, charts, or to make something stand out on the page. Never mix more than two types of fonts on a page; even though it is tempting to be wild and crazy; the effect is busy, confusing, and unprofessional.

The CTRL F8 menu allows you to select sizes and attributes of fonts without going to the list of fonts and selecting every time. It is much more effective to use size and attribute because it is faster. If, at a later time, you decide to change the base font of the document, it will not be necessary to change all the sizes and attributes. In other words, **large** will always be the large font, regardless of the base font. This is the same idea as the Style--a change will be a global change. It is not necessary to ferret out every font size or attribute code and change them if you change the base font.

To determine what the size and attribute fonts are for the default font, use the PTR program. At the DOS C prompt, type *PTR HPLASEII.PRS*, or whatever PRS file that you are using. When the printer is highlighted, press **ENTER**, highlight Fonts, press **ENTER**, highlight the default font, press **ENTER**, highlight Automatic Font Changes, press **ENTER**. This screen will tell you what fonts will be used for large, italics, and so on. It is possible to change these, but do so with caution. The program selects the most appropriate fonts for the sizes and attributes that are **available**. Unless you are graphically artistic, you should probably leave well enough alone. It is useful to have a copy of this page, so do a screen dump to the printer. (Depending upon the type of keyboard you have, use either SHFT PrtSc or just the Print Screen key. The Print Screen will be used alone if it is on an enhanced keyboard will lots of extra keys, so that it is not used for anything else. You can screen-dump to any printer by using this command, just remember that it prints everything that you see on the screen, and that lines will probably appear printed as alpha characters.)

CREATING A HEADER (OR A FOOTER)

What you do	What you will get

Step   **The header**
1

1.	SHFT F8, 2 [P], 3 [H], 1 [A], 2 [P], SHFT F5, 2 [C], ALT F6, CTRL B, F7, F7	Creates a header on every page which places the date on the left and the page number flush right. Notice that the date code is used so that the date will automatically be the current date when printed.

NOTE: There are two choices for headers, A and B. You can actually create two different headers. If you do that, make sure that the second does not go on top of the first. Usually one, perhaps A, would be used for odd pages, 3 [O], and the other, B, would be for even pages, 4 [V]. Notice, too, on the header choice line that you have the option to suppress the header for that particular page; this is most often used for the first page of a document. Most of WP's features work for headers, such as font sizes and attributes, centering, lines. They can also be edited after the fact, SHFT F8, 2 [P], 3 [H], 1 [A], 5 [E]. If you use REVEAL CODES you will be able to see the first 50 characters of the header. **Footers** are treated exactly the same as headers, except that they appear at the bottom of the page. If possible, create these in the beginning stages of the document, so that you have an idea of how the top and bottom margins will be affected.

Some examples:
A Footer

The CODES: [HLine:Left & Right, 4.38", 0.01", 100%] [AdvDn:0.2"] [SMALL] [ITALC]SCT BOCES SLS[Cntr][Date:3 1, 4][C/A/Flrt][Flsh Rt]^B[italc][small][C/A/Flrt][HRt] [HRt]

A Header Example.

The CODES:
Figure:1;AIRPLANE.WPG;][AdvToPos:4.33"][LARGE]New Acquisitions at the Library[large][HRt][AdvDn:0.3"][HLine:Left & Right,4.33",0.1",40%]

A Footer.

The CODES:
[Figure:1;AIRPLANE.WPG;][AdvToPos:4.33"][AdvDn:1.5"][LARGE]Ne w Acq at the Lib[large][AdvDn:0.3"][HLine:Left & Right,6.5",0.1",40%]

NOTE: When you create graphic boxes in headers and footers, the type should be paragraph. The result:

New Acquisitions at the Library

A Header

The Library

The Information Place

The CODES: [HLine:Left,4",0.01",100%][AdvDn:0.3"][EXT LARGE]The Library[ext large][HRt] The Information Place[AdvDn:0.3"][HLine:Left,4",0.01",100%][AdvToPos:4"][HLine:4 ",2.44",0.08",40%]

A Header, Column Headings

SCT BOCES School Library System Telephone Directory

Librarian	School	In Library	Number	Hours to Call
LaPier, Cynthia . SCT BOCES ... yes			739-3581	8 - 4:30

The CODES: [LARGE][ITALC]SCT BOCES School Library System Telephone Directory[HRt]Librarian[Tab]School[Tab]In Library[Tab]Number[Tab][Tab]Hours to Call[italc][large][HRt]Hours to Call[AdvDn:0.2"][HLine:Left & Right, 4.38",0.01",100%][italc][large][HRt]

It may be necessary to adjust the tabs after the columns are actually created.

CREATING A MACRO THAT PRINTS A MEMO

	What you do	What you will get
Step 1	**Defining the macro**	

1. CTRL F10, ALT Q, a macro to create a memo, ENTER, *MEMO*, ENTER, ENTER, *To:*, TAB, TAB, CTRL PG-UP, P, ENTER, ENTER, *From:*, TAB, TAB, *Cynthia*, ENTER, ENTER, *Re:*, TAB, TAB, CTRL PG-UP, P, ENTER, ENTER, *Date:*, TAB, TAB, SHFT F5, 2 [C], ENTER, ENTER, ENTER, CTRL F10

    Creates a macro that will be called up with ALT Q. The ALT key can be used in combination with any key which you will remember easily and which has not already been used for a macro. The macro will pause and allow the user to enter the To, and Re information followed by Enter. You can insert more hard returns if you want a different kind of spacing. Do this and give it to your secretary on her birthday--it is a neat gift!

2. CTRL F10, ALT Y, SHFT F7, N, 2, ENTER, 2 [P], HOME, HOME, HOME, ↑, CTRL-PG-DOWN, Y, CTRL F10

    Prints two copies of the page, goes to the beginning of the document, clears the screen.

CREATING A SHADED BOX

What you do   What you will get

Step   **Defining the box options**
1

1.   **ALT F9, 4 [U], 4 [O], 3 [I], .3, ENTER, .3, ENTER, .3, ENTER, .3, ENTER, 9 [G], 50, ENTER, F7, ALT F9, 4 [U], 1 [C], 3 [T], 2 [a], 4 [V], 5 [S], 2, ENTER, 5 [H], 3 [S], 1, ENTER, 6 [S], 3 [B], 1, ENTER, 1, ENTER, 8 [E], CTRL F8, 1 [S], 6 [V], 1, F7, F7**

Defines the options for the box, accepts the default of no lines around the edges of the box, makes the shading 50% black, which is really just another way of saying gray. The inside margin of the box is set for .3"; this may need to be changed later. It depends upon the size of the default font that you are using and what the very large is in actuality. Creates a box that is placed on the page, rather than connected with a paragraph. Notice that all the measurements are used as increments of one-inch; this is just to make it easier to remember. Finally, a large number is entered in the box.

2.   Highlight [Usr Box:1;;], **ALT F4**, move cursor to right of code, **CTRL F4, 1 [B], 2 [C], ENTER, SHFT F10, ENTER** (Repeat twice for four boxes in toto.)

Copies the box so that there are now four boxes. If you use SHFT F7, V to look at the boxes you will only see one, because they are all defined to be in the same position and will just sit on top of one another. If you copy too many boxes, just highlight the extra(s), and delete with the delete key.

3.   **ALT F9, 4 [U], 2 [E], 2, ENTER, 4 [V], 5 [S], 4,**

Now it is necessary to edit the boxes so that they are moved

	ENTER, 8 [E], delete #, replace with 2, F7, F7	down the page. After editing the second box, use SHFT F7, V to look at your creation. Instant gratification is very important to all of us. To edit boxes three and four, follow the same steps, increasing the vertical location by 2", and by increasing the number within the box by one.

NOTE: When editing boxes place the cursor on the box code in Reveal Codes, then it is not necessary to tell the program which box you want to edit; it knows. If the boxes do not fit on the page, it may be necessary to adjust the top and bottom margins. This all depends upon what you want to do with these nifty little creations.

4.	ALT F7, 4 [D], 1 [T], 2 [P], 4 [M] 1, ENTER, 3, ENTER 4, ENTER, ENTER, ENTER, 3 [C]	Sets up parallel columns, the first column will actually be empty because the box will be there.
5.	SHFT F8, 4 [O], 1 [A], 2 [D], 1.5, ENTER, 1 [A], 2 [D], 1.5, ENTER, 1 [A], 2 [D], 1.5, ENTER, 1 [A], 2 [D], 1.5, ENTER, F7	Sets up the advance positions so that the columns will be lined up with the boxes.
6.	CTRL ENTER, enter text after each Advance code.	Leaves the first columns blank, enters text after codes, so that it will appear in the correct position. The following page shows the results of this exercise.

131

1   *Weeding increases circulation.*

2   *MARC records are essential for successful conversion.*

3   *Standardization will be important for future growth.*

4   *Initially, automation costs LOTS of money.*

CREATING A MASTER DOCUMENT

	What you do	What you will get
Step 1	**Defining the master document**	
1.	**ALT F5, 2 [S], filename**	On a blank screen, each chapter or sub-document filename is loaded into the master document. The names do not have to be connected in any way. In other words, they do not have to be: Chap1, Chap2, etc.
2.	**Before each subdoc, CTRL-ENTER, SHFT F8, 2 [P], 2 [o], 1 [O], F7**	Each subdoc will start with a new page which is odd.
3.	**ALT F5, 6 [G], 3 [E]**	The document is expanded. All of the complete files are loaded. If each file has formatting codes, those codes are in effect until changed by later codes.
4.	**ALT F5, 6 [G], 4 [o]**	This condenses the master document back to its filename form. All of the editing changes that have been made during expansion will be saved if you so choose. If the file is saved as an expanded file, and not condensed, you will not be able to condense it again.

NOTE: When saving the master document shell, use .MAS as an extension to avoid confusion. Tables of contents and indexes should be generated after the document has been expanded. The document cannot be printed unless it is first expanded. Any document of several sections should be created using this feature. The individual files are shorter and easier to deal with.

CREATING A MACRO TO USE A STYLE

What you do	What you will get

Step 1   **Defining the macro**

1.   **CTRL F10, ALT X**, style-header, **ENTER, ALT F8, N**, header, **ENTER, 1 [O], CTRL F10**

Although the WP documentation does not reveal this fact, a style can be retrieved with N(ame), which is used exactly as it is with the F5 directory name search. In a Macro, the name command can be used to indicate a specific style without moving the cursor. Moving the cursor is ineffective, because every time a style is added or deleted the number of moves the cursor would make changes. The style is then turned on. All macros should be created only for those features that are used frequently enough to remember their existence.

135

CREATING BULLETS, GRAPHICALLY

What you do   What you will get

Step   Defining the box
1

1.   **ALT F9, 4 [U], 4 [O], 1**   Defines the options for the box,
        [B], 2 [S], 6 [T], 2 [S],   which will be that the top and
        6 [T], F7   left sides will be single lines, and
                                         the right and bottom will be thick
                                         lines. The thick can be changed
                                         to extra thick if you decide you
                                         need a bigger box; if the box is
                                         too small, extra thick will be
                                         overwhelming.

2.   **ALT F9, 4 [U], 1 [C], 5**   Creates a box that is .3' by .3'.
        [H], 1 [L], 6 [S], 3 [B],   This size can be changed to suit
        .3, ENTER, .3, ENTER,   your needs. Notice that the type
        F7   of box is paragraphical, and that
                                         it is positioned on the left.

3.   **ALT F4, highlight the box**   As has been done before, the box
        code, CTRL F4, 1 [B], 2   is   highlighted   and   copied.
        [C]   Depending upon the size of the
                                         box, it will be necessary to place
                                         hard return codes (try three)
                                         between each box to make them
                                         line up. (Try this without the
                                         hard returns; the effect is
                                         interesting and may inspire you
                                         to Michelangelic work.)

4.   **SHFT   F10,   ENTER,**   An easy method to copy the
        repeat as many times as   boxes. As with all duplicated
        you needs box.   boxes, each box will have to be
                                         edited for a specific position on
                                         the page. returns between each
                                         box code.

NOTE: Another method of creating a bullet is to leave the user defined box border option at the default, and change the 9 [G] to 100% to create a solid black bullet. All other steps will be exactly the same. These bullets can be mixed on a page. Just remember that the option will affect all of the following bullets until it is changed again.

CREATING A REPORT COVER SHEET

	What you do	What you will get
Step 1	**Setting the box options**	
1.	**ALT F9, 1 [F], 4 [O], 1 [B], 7 [E], 7 [E], 7 [E], 7 [E], F7**	Creates options for a box with extra thick sides.
2.	**ALT F9, 1 [F], 1 [C], 3 [T], 2 [a], 4 [V], T, 5 [H], 1 [M], 3 [C], 6 [S], 3 [B], 6.17, ENTER, 8.83, ENTER, 7 [W], NO, F7**	Creates an empty box which is of the page type and is located at the top of the page centered between the margins. Not wrapping text around will allow another box to be superimposed on this box.
3.	**ALT F9, 1 [F], 4 [O], 1 [B], 3 [D], 3 [D], 3 [D], 3 [D], 3 [I], .25, ENTER, .25, ENTER, .25, ENTER, .25, ENTER, F7**	Creates a box option that has double lined sides and a .25" inside margin.
4.	**ALT F9, 1 [F], 1 [C], 3 [T], 2 [a], 4 [V], 5 [S], 2, ENTER, 5 [H], 1 [M], 3 [C], 6 [S], 3 [B], 5, ENTER, 1.43, ENTER, 8 [E], CTRL F8, 1 [S], 7 [E], SHFT F6, *THE EMPIRE LIBRARY*, ENTER, SHFT F6, *ANNUAL REPORT*, ENTER, SHFT F6, *1989*, F7, F7**	Creates a box that will *sit* inside the first box. This one is another page type, is centered between the margins, but is established in a specific position, 2" from the top of the page. The text is entered in an extra large font and is centered on the lines.

THE EMPIRE LIBRARY

ANNUAL REPORT

1989

CREATIVITY WITH TABS

What you do   What you will get

Step **Tabs with leaders, or little**
1   **dots**

1.   **SHFT F8, 1 [L], 8 [T],**   Will automatically place dot
     HOME, HOME, ←, place   leaders every time the tab is
     a **.** on every tab setting, pressed. See below.
     F7, F7

School . . . . Grade level
Riverside K-6
Southside 9-12

NOTE: This would be useful for a phone directory or any list that is read across and has a tendency to be confusing, when in the landscape mode.

Step **Tabs with underlines**
2

2.   **SHFT F8, 4 [O], 7 [U],**   Will underline whenever a tab is
     YES, YES, F7, F8   used. See below.

Name_____

School_____

Address_____

Phone_____ Fax_____

NOTE: This is great for creating forms. Even though horizontal lines will create the same thing, this method is really easy and does not require any measuring!

CREATING A THREE-FOLD PAMPHLET

What you do   What you will get

Step 1	Defining the page and columns

1. **SHFT F8, 2 [P], 8 [S], 2 [t], 1 [S], F7, ALT F7, 4 [D], 2 [N], 3, ENTER, 3 [D], 1, ENTER, F7, 3 [C]**

The paper size and perspective will be 11 x 8.5, landscape. The brochure will have three columns with an inch between columns for folding. Column mode is turned on. The following steps are based on a fold that goes from right to middle, and left to middle. The left becomes the top sheet, the right becomes the second sheet.

2. Enter text.

The codes for this pamphlet are shown below. It is sometimes necessary to change the font size with each panel to *make* the text fit within the space. The pages following the codes are the pamphlet itself.

NOTE: If you make an error in the layout, and an inside panel should be on page 2; use the ALT F4 to block a column, CTRL F4, 2 [C] to move an entire column and leave the rest of the columns intact.

Library Automation

A Workshop for Librarians and Library Administrators

May 5, 6, 1989

Elmira, NY
Mark Twain Center
Quarry Farm

sponsored by the School Library System, SCT BOCES and the Steele Memorial Public Library

For more detailed directions, please call the Quarry Farm, (607) 333-2222, 8am - 12 pm, Mon - Thurs. Scenic tours will be available upon request. Mark Twain's ghost does inhabit the farm, please do not bring impressionable children to the conference.

WHO

A panel of librarians with extensive automation experience, positive and negative, constructive and destructive, will discuss the what's and wherefore's of library automation. Small groups will prepare action plans and develop grant proposals.

WHOM

The workshop will be for librarians who are interested in implementing automation projects and for administrators who supervise librarians who are interested in automating their libraries. It will be assumed that all participants will know what a MARC record is and why; and have a basic understanding of the microcomputer.

WHERE

The workshop will be held in the computer room at the glorious Mark Twain Center. The computer room has available a local area network for hands-on experience.

AGENDA

9:00 - 9:15 Registration, coffee

9:15 - 9:45 Welcome address, Librarian Jones

9:45 - 10:30 Panel Presentation: Data Preparation

10:30 - 11:15 Panel Presentation: System Evaluation

11:15 - 12:00 Panel Presentation: System Installation

12:00 - 1:15 Lunch, dessert and drink included

1:15 - 3:30 Three concurrent small group workshops: Grant Proposals, Automation Action Plans, Training

Presenters

Librarian Jones - Ms. Jones has had twenty years of library automation experience, beginning with the card catalog in third grade, and presently with the automated system at Empire Library.

Susie Smith - librarian, Cornell University, established the first academic - public school link in New York State

Other automation librarians

REGISTRATION

The deadline for registration is April 16, 1989. Please enclose $25 workshop fee with registration to guarantee a seat. A Continuing Education credit will be offered for an additional $50.

NAME
LIBRARY
ADDRESS
PHONE

Send registration to
Empire Library
ATTN: Automation Workshop
3 Library Plaza
Elmira, NY
14903-2333

143

CREATING MATH COLUMNS

What you do   What you will get

Step 1 | **Setting the tabs, by creating styles**

1. | **ALT F8, 3 [C], 1 [N] TABS-NORMAL, ENTER, 2 [T], 2 [O], 4 [C], SHFT F8, 1 [L], 8 [T], F7, F7, 6 [S], F7** | Accepts and sets up a normal tab setting, every half-inch and left aligned, which can be returned to after a block of math has been done. This minimizes confusion with tabs because it establishes two types: normal and math. You will almost always be able to use one or the other without modification.

2. | **ALT F8, 3 [C], 1 [N] TABS-MATH, ENTER, 2 [T], 2 [O], 4 [C], SHFT F8, 1 [L], 8 [T], CTRL END, L and then at every inch increment, ., F7, F7, F7, F7, 6 [S]** | Creates a style for math tabs, which leaves the tab at 0" as a left aligned tab, and sets up a right decimal aligned tab every inch.

Step 2 | **defining the math columns**

3. | **ALT F7, 2 [e]**, {cursor will be blinking on 2}, move cursor to columns **B, 0, A*.27, ENTER, 0, B+23446, F7, 1 [M]** | Establishes the columns for math with a formula in column B which will multiply the amount in A by $.27. Column B will then add the result, which is column B, to 23446. Finally turn the math feature on.

NOTE: If for any reason you need to edit the math columns definition, using Reveal Codes place the cursor after the [MathDef] code and use ALT F7, 2 [e]. As long as the cursor is after the definition code, then the formulas, etc., will reflect those that you established the first time. If you change a column out of order, WP is able to deal with the change even though the formulas may look out of order.

4.	Move cursor to the beginning of the document, before the math codes, type *SCHOOL*, TAB, TAB, *ITEMS*, TAB, TAB, *COST*, TAB, TAB, *TOTAL*, move the cursor until it is at the end of all the codes.	Sets up your headings before the math codes so that they are not right aligned. The tab settings may need to be adjusted slightly to match the math columns, but if the tabs are one-half an inch and the math columns are one-inch, two tabs should make the columns line up properly. To start to enter math data, it is necessary to move the cursor to a point beyond the math definition and the code for math on.
5.	ENTER, ENTER, *Riverside*, TAB, *2345*, TAB, TAB, ENTER, *Broadway*, TAB, *4567*, TAB, TAB, ENTER, *Diven*, TAB, TAB, ENTER, ENTER, TAB, +, TAB, DELETE !, +, TAB, DELETE !, +	Enter data, enter tabs to establish where the calculations will take place. On the last line, the +'s will add the columns vertically.
6.	ALT F7, 2 [a]	Causes the calculations.

NOTE: If you want to use a tab without the math calucation occuring, just delete the !. The !'s and +'s will not show up when printed. The above example should look like the following (on your screen):

School	Items	Cost	Total
Riverside	2345	633.15!	24,079.15!
Broadway	4567	1,233.09!	24,679.09!
Diven	8967	2,421.09!	25,867.09!
	15,879.00+	4,287.33+	74,625.33+

NOTE: The +'s and !'s show up in the above example because the file was imported into SideKick and then retrieved within this document. The reason for using SK is that in order to show the +'s and !'s, it is necessary to use a program other than WP. WP will recognize these as characters which are not to be printed, SK doesn't care what they are beyond the fact that they are characters.

CREATING A BAR GRAPH

What you do   What you will get

Step **Defining tabs**
1

1.   SHFT F8, 1 [L], 8 [T],   Sets up the tabs so that the first
      delete tab settings at half- *column* has plenty of space.
      inch intervals, F7,   Entitles the page with a style that
      ENTER, ENTER, ALT   is large and bold. If necessary the
      F8, (7 [R], BOOKS.STY),   style is retrieved.
      highlight *heading*,
      ENTER, *Interlibrary Loan*
      Statistics 1988-89, →

2.   *JULY*, TAB, ALT F9, 5   Enters July statistics. Starts the
      [L], 1 [H], 1 [H], 5 [S],   line at the position of the cursor
      2, ENTER, 2 [L], .5,   after the tab, which is 2" inches,
      ENTER, 3 [W], .25,   creates a line that is .25" wide. If
      ENTER, ENTER   every inch represents 500
                                    interlibrary loan transactions, then
                                    .5" would be about 250.

3.   For August through Dec,   Reading the codes, you are able
      enter the month, TAB,   to determine that the line is
      and the following lines: horizontal, 2" from the edge of
      AUGUST[Tab][HLine:2"   the page. The next measurement
      ,0.5",0.25",100%] [HRt]   is the length of the line. The
      S   E   P   T   width of the line is .25". All lines
      [Tab][HLine:2",2",0.25",   are 100% gray, or black. After
      100%][HRt]   each line, strike enter twice to
      OCT[Tab][HLine:2",3",0   leave a blank line.
      .25",100%][HRt]
      NOV[Tab][HLine:2",3.5"
      ,0.25",100%][HRt]
      DEC[Tab][HLine:2",4",0
      .25",100%][HRt]

4.   ENTER, type *# ILL*   Creates a key for graph

147

transactions, at every inch increment type *0, 500, 1500*, etc.

comprehension. The result should be as follows:

Interlibrary loan statistics, 1988-89

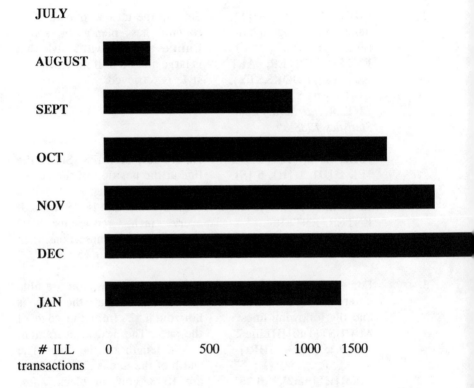

	0	500	1000	1500

ILL transactions

CREATING A CALLOUT

What you do   What you will get

**Step   Placing the callout
1**

1.   (Retrieve a text file), **ALT F9, 3 [B], 4 [O], 1 [B], 1 [N], 1 [N], 6 [T], 6 [T], 9 [G], 0, ENTER, F7, ALT F4,** highlight whatever text to be included in the callout, **CTRL F4, 1 [B], 2 [C], ALT F9, 3 [B], 1 [C], 3 [T], 2 [a], 4 [V], 3, 5 [H], 1 [M], 3 [C], 6 [S], 3 [B], 1.5, 1.5, 8 [E], ENTER, F7, F7**

Creates a box option that will give you a box with thick top and bottom lines and no background. Blocks the text which is to be the callout. Creates a box which is placed on the page, retrieves the blocked text. You may need to make some adjustments on the size and the location of the box, depending upon the document. It is also appropriate to make the text 2 point sizes larger than the rest of the document, or to use italics or bold. The purpose of the callout is to draw the reader's attention, but at the same time not detract from the looks of the document.

Among the primary reasons for standardizing with Marc is the transportability of records.

CREATING A MASTHEAD WITH AN ADDRESS OR MOTTO

What you do   What you will get

Step **Creating the masthead**
1

1. **ALT F9, 1 [F], 4 [O], 1**   Sets the figure box option so that
    [B], 2 [S], 2 [S], 2 [S],   the box has a single line border
    2 [S], 6 [C], delete   on all sides and so that the
    Figure, **ENTER, F7**   caption is not related to any
                                         numbering system.

2. **ALT F9, 1 [F], 1 [C], 1**   Creates the box, loads a graphic.
    [F], BORDER.WPG,   The border is part of the WP
    ENTER, delete box   package, in reality the logo should
    number code, **CTRL F8,**   be related to the institution in
    1 [S], 4 [S], CTRL F8, 2   some fashion. The caption is
    [A], 4 [I], SHFT F6, enter   entered in small italics and
    text: *School Library System*   centered underneath the box.
    SCT BOCES 431 Philo Rd.
    Elmira, NY, **F7**

3. **3 [T], 2 [a], 5 [H], 1**   Defines the graphic as being of
    [M], 3 [C], 6 [S] 3 [B],   the page type and located at the
    4, ENTER, 2, ENTER, 7   top and centered. The box size is
    [W], N, F7   arbitrary, and may be adjusted.
                                         The choice of *N* for wrapping text
                                         will allow you to enter text within
                                         the border.

4. **SHFT F8, 4 [O], 1 [A],**   Advances the text to the exact
    2 [D], 1.5, ENTER, F7,   position so that it will appear
    CTRL F8, 1 [S], 6 [V],   inside of the border. Sets the
    SHFT F6, enter text: *The*   parameters of large and centered
    Flyer   for the text.

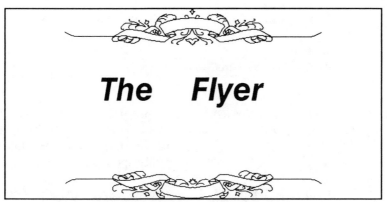

School Library System SCT BOCES 431 Philo Rd. Elmira NY

CREATING A GRID FOR AN ACTION PLAN

	What you do	What you will get
Step 1	**Defining the columns**	
1.	SHFT F8, 2 [P], 8 [S], 2 [t], 1 [S], F7	Although it is possible to do this in the portrait mode, it is much easier to understand in the landscape mode.
2.	ALT F7, 4 [D], 1 [T], 2 [P], 2 [N], 7, ENTER, F7, 3 [C]	Creates seven columns, one for each of the six months involved and one for the committees. Be sure to change the margins before this step if you intend to change the margins, so that WP will automatically figure the columns.
3.	ALT F9, 5 [L], 2 [V], 1 [H], 3 [B], ENTER, ENTER. Repeat increasing one column for each 3 [B].	Creates the vertical lines and attaches them to the columns. Lines cannot be edited so this step must be repeated for each column. If you try to create a line for column 7, WP will ignore it.
4.	Enter text, see example. At the end of the line, CTRL-ENTER.	Text is entered as in any parallel column example. The next step should be used after a complete line of text has been entered.
5.	ALT F9, 5 [L], 1 [H], 1 [H], 5 [S], 1, ENTER, 2 [L], 9, ENTER, F7, SHFT F8, 4 [O], 1 [A], 2 [D], .5, ENTER, F7	Creates a horizontal line to separate committees, advances the text .5" to prevent striking over text. These codes can be blocked and retrieved with

152

ENTER, and SHFT F10, ENTER
for each horizontal line.

	July	August	Sept	Oct	Nov	Dec	
Public Relations		design promo	get approval	print	distribute	evaluate	finalize project
Registration		gather program info	plan packet	design	print	distribute	tally registrations
Program		brainstorm ideas	select programs	gather proposals	select programs	contact pre-senters	evaluate

CREATING SPECIAL CHARACTERS

What you do   What you will get

Step   Defining the characters
1

1.	**S H F T F 1 0 ,** **CHARMAP.TST**	Retrieves the document that will show what special characters are available for your hardware configuration, specifically the printer.
2.	**CTRL 2, 5, 7, ENTER**	☺ will show on the screen. If you put the cursor on the character, reveal codes (ALT F3) will show the code that was used to get this happy face. If a ` appears, the printer is not capable of reproducing that character. Remember, the CTRL 2 is followed by the character set #, a comma, and the number of the character.

NOTE: Some of the character sets include letters with foreign accent marks. This is a much easier way to include these little pesky marks, for example, ƙ æ ç. WP calls the CTRL 2 command *compose*. Compose also allows you to type two letters together to create one character, æ (ae), ö ("o). CTRL V accomplishes the same thing, asking for a key which is the character set #, comma, the character number.

CREATING A MERGE FILE

What you do   What you will get

Step 1 **The secondary file**

Map out your plan: the file will be used for bibliographic records, that is, acquisition lists, order forms, shelf list cards, simple subject bibliographies. It will not be used as a replacement for the card catalog, but just as a temporary print-out until the cards are received from the jobber or to let patrons know what is new.

For this example, use the following field concepts:

last name, first name   title
place of publication   publisher
date   call number
subject   ISBN
note field

1.   On a blank screen enter: *NAME*, F9, *TITLE*, F9, *PLACE*, F9, *PUBLISHER*, F9, *DATE*, F9, *CALL #*, F9, *SUBJECT*, F9, *ISBN*, F9, *NOTE FIELD*, F9

This creates a template record at the beginning of the file. You can always refer back to this to see just how you set up the fields. It also helps decrease confusion if more than one person is going to use the file.

2.   Now enter a real record:

Step 2 **An alternate method for creating the record format**

3.   ^R *01 NUM*, ^R *02 ISBN*, ^R *03 TYPE*, ^R *04 TITLE*, ^R *05 AUTHOR*, ^R *06 PUBLISHER*, ^R *07 COPYRIGHT*, ^R *08 DATE*, ^R *09 PRICE*,

Creates a template of fields for the primary file. The field numbers are not actually necessary, but will be helpful when setting up the merge files later.

^R *10 NOTES*

4.   Enter data followed by **F9**   Sets up a data file. It is necessary
0001 ^R   to include at least a ^R for every
^R   field number, even if the field
CS^R   itself contains no information. It
Crosstalk   XVI   is also necessary to mark the end
Communications   of a record with a ^E. The file
Software^R   should look exactly like this
^R   column. Saves the files as a
^R   secondary file with the extension
^R   .sf.
870723 ^R
50.00 ^R
^R
(At the end of the Record
use **SHFT F9, E**)
^E
0002 ^R
^R
vf ^R
Cornell University Audio
Visual   Catalog   1987-
88 ^R
^R
Cornell University ^R
^R
870709 ^R
00 ^R
^R
^E
0003 ^R
^R
vf ^R
Alerting   A   New
Audience about Teaching
as a Career ^R
^R
NYS Education Dept &
Council of State Chief
School Officers ^R

157

```
^R
870805 ^R
 00 ^R
^R
^E, F7, save the file as
acq.sf.
```

NOTE: If WP Library is used, the notebook program would be used to set up an input record which would look something like this:

ACQUISITIONS RECORDS FOR   1987-1988 SCT BOCES SLS

NUMBER	ISBN	TYPE

TITLE
AUTHOR
PUBLISHER
COPYRIGHT
DATE
PRICE
NOTES

If this is used, it is not necessary to enter the ^R and ^E codes. WP automatically enters them as data is input into this form. This is really the ideal way to enter data; it makes sense to everyone. Any staff person can easily learn how to input without extensive training in the use of WP.

5.   **SHFT F9, F, 5, ENTER, TAB, SHFT F9, F, 4, ENTER, TAB, SHFT F9, F, 7, ENTER,** save file as *acq.pf*   Sets up the fields for the merge: author, title, copyright date. Saves file as primary file. The use of .pf as part of the file name is conducive to less chaos in the workplace.

NOTE: The pf should look somewhat like this:
^F5^   ^F4^   ^F7^

It could be changed so that instead of each field being separated by a tab, a comma could be used:
^F5^, ^F4^, ^F7^

which would give a result closer to the bibliographic form with which we are all enamored. Again, it depends upon the use of the list. It is always possible to go back late and use search and replace and replace tabs with commas or vice versa.

6.	**SHFT F9, N, SHFT F9, P, SHFT F9, P**	Looks for the next record during the merge, and does not add a hard page at the end of each record.
7.	**CTRL F9, 1 [M], ACQ.PF, ENTER, ACQ.SF, ENTER**	Performs the merge.

NOTE: The next appropriate setup would be to sort the list, CTRL F9, 2 [S]. The result might look like the following:

American Bar Association, U.S Constitution Bicentennial, A We the People Resource Book, 1987
American Bar Association, We the People, A Handbook on Community Forums on the Constitution, 1987
Anderson, Eric S, Wired Librarian's Almanac, The, 1987
Ballard Thomas H, Failure of Resource Sharing in Public Libraries and...., 1986

This is an example with commas instead of tabs between each field. It has been sorted alphabetically. After the fact, it is apparent that it would have been appropriate to start the primary file with a F4, SHFT TAB to create an outdent; and to end the field line with a hard return so that there would be a space after each record. Fortunately, it is easy to make these corrections; just because the file has been merged does not mean that the data has been mutilated. Some other primary file possibilities for an acquisitions data file follow below:

THE PRIMARY FILE
^ F4 ^   ^ F3 ^   ^ F9 ^
^ N ^ P ^ P

THE CODES
[T   a   b
Set:0",0.5",1",4",4.5",5",5.5",6",6.5",7",7.5",8",8.5",9",9.5",10",10.5",11",11.5",1

2",12.5",13",13.5",14"][Math Def][Math On][Math
Def]^F4^[Tab]^F3^[Align]^F9^[C/A/Flrt][HRt]^N ^P ^P[HRt]
THE RESULT

Media Directory 1988	vf	$10.00
Subject Index to NY St	vf	
		$10.00
Image Builders		$10.00
Special Report:Publ	b	$12.00
Wheels for the mind	p	$12.00
Wisconsin Libr Media	bk	$13.00
Murder in the Stacks	vhs	$17.50

$84.50

When the merge was completed, the last line was added to calculate the
total. Another use of this list might be to sort by type of purchase (vf,
b, or vhs) and to create subtotals of each category. Sometimes the fields
do not line up properly and the math calculations are not correct. If that
occurs, go back to the beginning of the document and revise the tab
settings. The list will not be adversely affected even if this is done several
times.

OTHER MERGE OPTIONS

DATA FIELDS FOR AN INTERLIBRARY LOAN RECORD FILE

01 **TYPE** (book, copy, other)
02 **MONTH**
03 **REGION** (the consortium region)
04 **OUTSIDE** (the region)
05 **BORROWER**
06 **STATUS** (borrower-faculty, student, etc)
07 **LENDER**
08 **AUTHOR**
09 **TITLE**
10 **PERIODICAL**
11 **CITATION**

12 **REQUEST** date
13 **DUE** date
14 **FINISHED** date
15 **RECEIVED** date
16 **SENT** date
17 **3ITEM** received
18 **4PASSED** to borrowing library
19 **5ITEM** returned from borrower
20 **LIBRARY-TYPE** system, public, academic, etc
21 **NOTES** any additional information
22 **LOAN#** in-house number

These are just suggested fields. As a System, we have to keep track of more extensive statistics than the norm. This is an optimal example of how meaninglessly blown out of proportion statistics can become. Reports can be generated on this file based on:

> type of items transacted - how many books, copies, etc.
> type of libraries involved in transactions
> titles of items borrowed for collection development purposes
> transactions per month
> length of transactions
> transactions within and without of the consortium
> type of borrowers

to name just a few.

In most merge cases, it is necessary to do a sort after the merge. We usually evaluate statistics based on some kind of grouping (month, type, or whatever) which is easily accomplished by sorting.

PRIMARY FILES FOR MERGES

^F1^   ^F2^ ^F5^ ^F7^
^N ^P ^P
^Gmsort^G

RESULT

TYPE	MONTH	BORROWER	LENDER
C	07	LINTAL	VXE
C	07	LINTAL	VXE
C	07	LINTAL	VYQ
C	07	LINTAL	VZH

NOTE: The header was added after the sort, otherwise it will show up as the header for every record. Using the sort feature this report can be sorted on all four columns and printed each time. This sort was done with a macro that was inserted into the primary file. *Msort* sets up a sort for the fields in order, 1,2,3,4, and performs the sort, after moving the cursor to the beginning of the file, of course.

THE MACRO
{DISPLAYOFF}{Home}{Home}{Home}{Up}{Merge/Sort}2{Enter}{
Enter}3a1{Right}1{Right}a2{Right}1{Right}a3{Right}1{Right}a4{Rig
ht}1{Exit}1

CREATING A MERGE FOR LABELS

What you do   What you will get

Step   **Setting up the address**
1   **secondary file**

1.   *NAME* ^R   Establishes the field for the
           TITLE ^R   address file. Remember the F9
           STREET ^R   key will produce the ^R
           CITY ^R   automatically.
           STATE ^R
           ZIP ^R

2.   Enter data. Follow each
           record with ^E.

3.   Save file, *address.sf.*

4.   ^F1^   Sets up and saves the format for
           ^F2^   the labels.
           ^F3^
           ^F4^, ^F5^ ^F6^
           ^N ^P ^P
           Save as *address.pf*

5.   CTRL   F9, 1 [M],   Executes the merge.
           ADDRESS.PF, ENTER,
           ADDRESS.SF, ENTER

6.   SHFT F7, S, 3 [E], 4 [F],   Defines as a printer form, labels.
           highlight All Others, 1   It should be necessary to do this
           [A], 4 [L], 5 [P], .25,   step only once.
           ENTER, .25, ENTER, F7
           until return to text screen

7.   SHFT F8, 2 [P], 8 [S], 0   Sets up the paper size for labels.
           [O], ENTER, ENTER, 4   Do this step after the merge, at
           [L]   the very beginning of the merged

163

file. N.B., this is for a non-laser printer and a single column label format.

Step 2	**a primary file for laser printer labels**	
8.	ALT F7, 4 [D], 1 [T], N, 2 [N], 3, 3 [D], .3, F7	Sets up column for the label format.
9.	SHFT F8, 1 [L], 4 [H], 2 [F], .15	Set up a line height which is fixed and is peculiar to laser labels.
10.	ALT F7, 3 [C]	Turns column feature on.
11.	SHFT F8, 4 [O], 1 [A], 2 [D], 1.35	Another eccentricity, advances down before label starts.
12.	^F2^ ^F1^ ^F5^ ^F6^ ^F7^ ^N, CTRL ENTER, ^F2^ ^F1^ ^F5^ ^F6^ ^F7^ ^N^P^P	Creates merge file for two column labels.
13.	For save and merge, follow steps 3 and 5 above.	

CONCLUSION

The essence in WordPerfect is the use of the program. It is okay to read about it, to understand the possibilities that go with it, but it is all for nothing if it is not put to use. So the most important step after perusing this book, is to go to the computer and try some of the examples, practice some of the steps. It does not do any good at all to say that the software is loaded on the machine, but that there is not time enough to learn how to use it. One has to make time.

Microcomputers are prolific in their availability. Laser printers are less than $1,000. Librarians really have to look far and wide for excuses to continue to use typewriters or unattractive dot matrix printers. All non-profit agencies should also accept the fact that to make money, you have to spend money. If two grant applications are submitted to a foundation, and one is slick, neat, and attractive, and the other is obviously corrected with white-out, not formatted at all, and unattractive, it is quite clear which application is seriously considered -- regardless of the content. The reader doesn't get to the content; the first impression is the one that has the greatest impact and gives the greatest credibility to a document.

When library patrons of all types are being exposed everyday to desktop published documents, librarians must accept the fact that the most attractive documents receive the most attention. If boards of trustees, Friends of the Library, administrators, and others are to believe and are to keep giving funds, the library's printed products must have the appearance of an inherent worth.

Finally in this day and age of technology, librarians in all types of libraries must model what we expect to be second nature for our patrons. We must offer to provide online searches on a disk instead of on paper, accompanied by some easy instructions on how to use that file with WordPerfect. We expect our patrons to need and request state-of-the-art reference services, to understand the need for specificity and Boolean logic, yet we deliver these services in the age old paper format. It is more than just automating the card catalog. If we show our patrons that we are as comfortable with the use of all of the other tools of technology as we expect them to be, then they will in turn become more comfortable and more adept at taking full advantage of the possibilities.

Regardless of the type of library involved, there are two aspects to be considered when planning library technology: management and instructional. Management covers the administrative and supervisory type

165

tasks; and instructional covers all the times that you spend at the "card catalog" helping the patron. It is equally important that we be concerned about both areas, and about the impact of technology on both. One area cannot be automated without the other. If we are using CD-ROMS as an ordering tool or as a database for literature searches for patrons, then we should be using word processors.

This book is only the beginning. Already WordPerfect 5.0 has moved on to 5.1, able to accomplish more, to take advantage of the mouse functions, and to be an even more sophisticated program approaching the desktop publishing level. The examples in this book are only the basics. With practice and more exposure to the program, it will soon become clear how the program can be used in many more ways. It will also become clear how many times the merge function or the style sheet or some other function can be used over and over with slight variations in all kinds of library situations.

The key is to do it, to use the software and to guide others in the use of the software. Our goal should not only be to answer all reference questions with 100% accuracy, but also to present an image of quality and perfection in all library areas.

SUGGESTIONS FOR FURTHER READING

Alderman, Eric. "WordPerfect Gets Better!" **PC WORLD 6:108-113 9/88**

Alsonso, Robert. "Buyer's Guide Expanded Listings." **PERSONAL COMPUTING 12:177-192 (9) 6/88**

Antonoff, Michael. "Word processors: Still Adding Power." **PERSONAL COMPUTING 12:139-175 (24) 6/88**

Archibald, Dale. "WordPerfect 5.0" **PC PUBLISHING 3:58-61 (3) 9/88**

Bedard, Patrick. "WordPerfect's Latest: Release 5.0" PC/COMPUTING 1:94-99 8/88

Bee, Harry. "Publish it on a Desktop." **PC RESOURCE #19:58-68 (10) 10/88**

__ "The Best Gets Better." **PC RESOURCE #21:147-148 12/88**

Blodgett, Ralph. "WordPerfect Desktop Publisher." **PC WORLD 6:138-139 5/88**

Crider, Janet. "Practically Perfect." **PUBLISH! 3:51-52 9/88**

Falk, Lawrence C. "WordPerfect 5.0 - Almost *Perfect* Upgrade." **PCM 6:100-102 9/88**

Flanders, Bruce. "WordPerfect 5.0 - Expanded Functionality and Complexity." **LIBRARY AUTOMATION 2:2-6 1/89**

Hannote, Dean. "WordPerfect on the Move." **PC MAGAZINE 7:117-143 (13) 12/29/88**

Howard, Bill. "The Best of 1988." **PC MAGAZINE 8:127-171 (26) 1/17/89**

Lombardi, John. "Executive Word Processors." **INFOWORLD 10:43-77 (20) 9/26/88**

__ "WordPerfect is Once Again King of the Hill." **INFOWORLD 10:67-70 (3) 6/20/88**

Marion, Craig. "Point/Counterpoint: Word vs. WordPerfect." **PERSONAL COMPUTING 12:127-134 (7) 5/88**

Mendelson, Edward. "WordPerfect 5.0: Was it Worth the Wait?" **PC MAGAZINE 7:48, 54 8/88**

Morgenstern Steve. "The Top Stars of Word Processing: WordPerfect and Microsoft Word." **HOME-OFFICE COMPUTING 7:49-53 1/89**

Nieburg, Hal. "An Exciting WordPerfect 5.0 Makes Its Debut." **COMPUTER SHOPPER 8:158+ (4) 5/88**

O'Malley, Christopher. "The Case for Power Word Processing." **PERSONAL COMPUTING 12:45, 47 10/88**

__ "Picture Perfect WordPerfect 5.0." **PERSONAL COMPUTING 12:165-166 8/88**

__ "Words and Graphics: Together at Last." **PERSONAL COMPUTING 12:137-144 (6) 11/88**

Pepper, Jon. "WordPerfect 5.0 Seamlessly Melds Text, Graphics." **PC WEEK 5:93, 98 6/21/88**

__ "The Point of It All." **PC CLONES 2:45-55 4/88**

Seymour, Jim. "The Most Important Products of 1988." **PC/COMPUTING 2:67-81 1/89**

__ "Great Looking Pages." **PC/COMPUTING 1:78-85 8/88**

Strehlo, Christine. "What's So Special About WordPerfect?" **PERSONAL COMPUTING 12:100-116 (14) 3/88**

Welsch, Erwin. "New Technologies." **SMALL COMPUTERS IN LIBRARIES 8:27-30 11/88**

Will-Harris, Daniel. "WordPerfect 5: Coming of Age." **PERSONAL PUBLISHING 4:74-83 (6) 9/88**

__ "WordPerfect 5: Roach Motel." **PERSONAL PUBLISHING 4:22 8/88**

INDEX

FUNCTION KEYS INDEX